A TEACHING HEART

Dear First Lady, Michelle OBAMA,

God Bless and Keep you.

Our children are our Hope
and we must teach them
with love, understanding
and courage.

Thoughtfully,
Dr. [signature]

A TEACHING HEART

A Notebook for Managing
Classrooms, Experiencing
Cultural Diversity For Effective
Teaching and Developing
Confident Parenting Skills

Ethlyn Davis Fuller, Ph.D.

To order additional copies of this book, contact:
Xlibris Corporation
1-888-795-4274
www.Xlibris.com
Orders@Xlibris.com
46516

CONTENTS

DEDICATION

A Teaching Heart is dedicated to my daughter, Chiara Davis Fuller.

She is a *special gift,* an adventurer, a courageous teacher, and an extraordinary person who continuously inspires and supports me and others in their life's journey.

To my parents, Ruth and Ernest Davis who loved me, believed in me, and encouraged me to "push the envelope" beyond the limits.

To my brothers, Ernest and John who have always been my "cheering section" in my making important decisions and living humbly.

To my students who over the years have given me the "permission" to teach and learn about student behaviors, curriculum, learning styles, multicultural diversity, and effective classroom instruction.

PROLOGUE

While on sabbatical from teaching at Cambridge College in Cambridge, Massachusetts, during 2006-2007 academic year, I was asked by a former phenomenal, talented graduate-student educator—who is now a vice principal in the high school—to visit his final class of the semester. It was his last class, and he wanted me to come and share information and thoughts about teaching. The students were first-year teachers at the Cambridge Rindge and Latin High School in Cambridge, Massachusetts. I was honored and anxious at the same time. I had not been teaching for a semester and was not quite sure if I would be effective in the classroom. I remember speaking with my magnificent and gifted daughter who was teaching and tutoring English in Japan (in the JET Program—Japanese Educators and Teachers Program) at the time and shared my anxiety with her in one of our frequent e-mail sessions. Her response back to me really affected me in wonderful ways. She said, "Mom, you will be just fine. You have a teaching heart." What a wonderful statement to make—daughter to mother. She was right.

I visited the class, shared my information, thoughts, and wisdom about classroom management; and the first-year teachers responded in a positive and respectful manner. It was so fulfilling. Teaching for a small period of time and extending to first-year teachers some information and listening to their observations and challenges within themselves. It was exhilarating. The teachers really wanted to be successful in the classroom. They cared about their students and had concerns about their students completing assignments, getting to class on time, and respecting themselves as well as the teachers teaching them.

Teachers need to demonstrate self-control, have a purpose and philosophy of education, respect for self and others (open mind-different mind), enjoy the teaching, have confidence and a style of teaching what I call "your signature" style. What does your teaching look like? How do you communicate, and how do you listen in the classroom?

Diversity among students in our classrooms appears to increase each year, and we wonder how we can meet each child's needs. The policy of inclusion means that we are likely to have children with physical, emotional, or mental disabilities. These children may require the aid of an assistant teacher or, at the very least, our understanding of their special needs and how to meet them. As we continue to integrate students from different cultural backgrounds, we need to be aware of potential language difficulties. Also, some cultures have ways of communicating and interacting that differ from traditional-school practice.

In some cases, differences among students are obvious, but often they are so subtle that we are unaware of them. Students have many ways of knowing, but we tend to teach them in the ways that we ourselves learn neglecting the kinesthetic or auditory learner. Unfortunately, teachers often interpret mismatches in learning styles between themselves and the students as a lack of ability on the part of the students.

A TEACHING HEART

Teachers and parents are given the awesome responsibilities for influencing and nurturing children for a lifetime. Those responsibilities of teaching and parenting provide the catalysts that children respond to in a myriad of ways. Whatever the input into the child will effect the output of who and what that child is and will become. Teaching and parenting are challenging roles in a child's lifetime as well as our own. "Yes, I can" attitudes for teachers and parents give us permission to surmount this together. Simply put, it is about the child—the children (teaching, learning, and parenting in a diverse world).

A Passion to Teach

Teaching has been a passion of mine for more than four decades. In teaching, there is always a new or reaffirmed learning for me as an educator. Teaching in my view is shared learning of experiences, ideologies, concepts, contextual information, and building community in the learning environment. Whether teaching on the elementary level, middle school, high school, undergraduate, or graduate level, students come to the classroom with a wealth of knowledge and information from past experiences and living life. It is important for me to validate and respect the students that gather in my classroom for teaching/learning. It is a collaboration; it is a contract; it is a promise; it is an understood venture that both instructor and student are present to enhance and enrich each other through shared resources, cognitive thought, and respect. How that occurs depends on the members of the class and the spoken and unspoken agenda presented.

ACKNOWLEDGEMENTS

Writing this book has been a labor of love and commitment to what I am passionate about: teaching, learning, and parenting. It has been a reflective journey in putting my thoughts together, committing myself to the actual outlining, writing, rewriting, proofreading, and countless hours of editing. I have come to know and understand that nothing in life is accomplished alone. With faith, love, and support of some marvelous people, I graciously say THANK YOU.

Chiara, my magnificent daughter, for her wonderfulness in supporting and cheering me on during the writing of the manuscript. She gave me the idea for the title in one of our conversations about teaching and learning in the classroom.

Portia Lassister, for being a spiritual support person, professional educator, and proofreader in the early stages of the writing process.

Lynnette Turner for being a friend, soul sister, second reader, and typist of the manuscript. She was encouraging, supportive, and most efficient with her time and amazing organizational skills. She creatively brought the manuscript to life.

Cheryl Warrick, a longtime friend, gifted artist, and book cover designer. The Gallery NAGA in Boston and directors Arthur Dion and Meg White who gave their time and sincere effort in helping me select the artwork cover.

My two brothers—Ernest M. Davis and John Colgan-Davis—for their love, support, and encouragement with the manuscript and daily living.

Phyllis McCarley Wood, for encouraging me in writing the manuscript and her steadfast friendship, frequent phone calls, and unconditional sisterly love.

Florence Grant and Inge Williams who have been quite special—special friends and being like family to me for many years.

Special thanks to a host of close friends for believing in my thoughts.

The parents' forum at St. Paul African Methodist Episcopal Church—especially Myra Rodriguez, Roberta Green, Ronda Martinez, Hazel and Marshall Stanton—who collectively and individually have been resourceful and steadfast with their participation in the group. To Rev. Dr. LeRoy Attles (pastor) and Dr. Henrietta Attles for their unwavering support of the parent group.

Cambridge College colleagues—Professor Lyda Peters and Dr. Sandra Bridwell—who shared professional experiences, personal dreams, hopes about parenting, growing stronger as African American women, and giving each other the encouragement to be true to one's self.

Former students, present students who gave me the permission to teach, learn, and share content/ideas, and expertise. For future students who bring the desire to know and question. This is a humble and never-ending journey, indeed.

A very special thank you to Lynn Moore, Liana Smith and Lorie Adams for their diligent and professional work along with the excellent editing and production team, who made the changes, edits and updates for the manuscript.

INTRODUCTION

Effective Teaching and Learning to Benefit Students

Effective teaching and learning in the classroom benefit students, instructors, parents/guardians, and administrators. Effective teaching involves planning for lessons, implementing lessons, building classroom community, establishing classroom culture, valuing individual/group learning, respecting differences/similarities of students, managing behaviors, and understanding/demonstrating effective teaching and learning techniques using critical-thinking techniques for successful learning experiences in the classroom. In thinking about teaching and learning for students/teachers there is a laundry list of what to do and not do to attain and maintain classroom success. Before what to do and not to do can be addressed, it is important to cite the elements of effective teaching.

Get students emotionally involved to be passionate about the topic being taught. Model teachers use these methods to involve students emotionally.

Getting Students Emotionally Involved

The best learning takes place when people are passionate about the topic. Model teachers use these methods to involve students emotionally.

1. Ask students how they feel about what you just taught.
2. Use humor in the presentation.
3. As often as possible, demonstrate the passion that brought you into teaching.
4. Frequently use quotes from great people.
5. Ask students to memorize quotes from great people.
6. Regardless of what you teach, from time to time read or recite poetry about overcoming adversity. On any given day, some students need to hear it.

7. Use positive examples of students' past successes to generate an "I can do this" feeling.
8. Include in your curriculum people, events, experiences, and perspectives that reflect the cultures of your students.
9. Incorporate students' experiences into your assignments (Bell 2002; 2003, 34).

Meeting the Needs of Students Who Learn in Different Ways

How can we best meet the needs of students who learn in different ways? Try to recognize their learning styles and make lesson variations to fit those styles. We need to be aware that students are different and don't learn in the same ways or at the same pace. Then we need to apply what we have learned about them to our teaching. Allow time for self-discovery or self-directed learning. Provide different types of activities and teaching methods. Keep checking yourself until it becomes second nature to include different ways that students learn. Identify their ways in which a student learns best and teach him or her in that way. Provide students with variety of materials that they can choose from to best help them learn (Perry-Ross 1998, 21).

If we want our students to be able to think and understand, we need to address their strengths and offer them different ways of knowing. (Perry-Ross, 1998, 22)

A Hierarchy of Needs

Maslow's hierarchy of needs is a model to understand and incorporate into the teaching and learning environment. The needs of students and personnel related to the learning environment, i.e., teachers, parents, administrators, counselors, community workers, community agencies, religious institutions, social-service agencies, and the like include these five levels. Each level is important. Each level states what individuals need to achieve and maintain for their daily existence. The levels are important to maintain while achieving new levels for an individuals' well being.

If one or more levels are threatened or lost then that makes achieving in and out of the classroom more difficult. There is a correlation between meeting the needs of students who learn in different ways and Maslow's Hierarchy of needs. It is educating the "whole person" using a myriad of teaching techniques while being sensitive to the well-being of the individual.

Level 1 food, shelter, and clothing
Level 2 touch, interaction (verbal/nonverbal)
Level 3 acknowledgement
Level 4 safety/security
Level 5 self-actualization (realizing what you have obtained)

CHAPTER ONE

Effective Classroom Management

Effective classroom management is providing a "safe" place or students to experience the learning and sharing of ideas, feelings and perceptions.

—Dr. Beverly D. Tatum

Classroom management is respecting and valuing individuals in the learning environment. Classroom management is being responsible while teaching students. Classroom management is acknowledging differences and similarities in a supportive and nonjudgmental manner. Classroom management is allowing for success and failures without harming self-esteem in students. Classroom management is trust building. Classroom management is enabling the teacher to learn and experience teaching styles that challenge learning. Concretely stated, classroom management is the manner in which curriculum is taught, how students are treated, and how teachers teach. It is the scheduling of activities with emphasis on student abilities, as well as capabilities, motivation, and interest in learning. It is also the monitoring of class activities. Classroom management is the interchange of ideas, sharing of resources, and acknowledging of abilities and capabilities in the learning environment by teachers and students. Classroom management is including parents/guardians in classroom activities and child development issues and progress in the learning environment.

Effective classroom management is providing a *safe* place for students to experience the learning and sharing of ideas, feelings, and perceptions. Dr. Beverly Daniel Tatum writes, "It is assumed that in a society where racial group membership is emphasized, the development of racial identity will occur in some form in everyone. Given the dominant/subordinate relationship of whites and people of color in this society, however, it is not surprising that this development process will unfold in different ways. An understanding of these issues can help a teacher better think about classroom strategies for facilitating student discussions and promoting critical thinking." Dr. Tatum, a clinical psychologist and president of Spellman College in Atlanta, Georgia, advocates the use of a journal in and out of class so a student can see the evolution of his or her thinking, and the teacher can better understand the student's ideas. Also, providing reading materials and classroom situations where students can compliment their thinking and acquire new information about subject matter being discussed helps connect student ideas with content. Finally, Dr. Tatum believes students should be encouraged to discover how they can make a difference in their own lives and responsibly participate as citizens in a democracy (Stoskpf 1991. 10, 11).

What Effective Teaching Provides

Effective teaching provides for activities planned and implemented in the classroom that meet the criteria for the curriculum design and the student needs so that learning occurs. There is interaction and expectations for both students and teachers. There are goals and objectives for lessons and classroom learning. There are building classroom communities that involve parents, guardians, counselors, support staff, and instructional aides.

There are classroom cultures (the way the learning environment promotes learning/valuing of individuals) that encompass and respect (or acknowledge) individual behaviors, needs, and group dynamics. There are the elements of valuing individual and group learning. Those elements are respect, acknowledgement of strengths and weakness, listening and hearing what each other says, and deferring judgments. There are elements that are teaching critical thinking and problem solving. There is the managing of various behaviors and learning styles in the classroom. Managing classroom behavior is the opposite of controlling classroom behavior. To control a classroom is a monumental and self-depreciating experience. Controlling suggest that the teacher is the dominate factor, and all must comply to a single direction with negative/positive consequences if not followed by the students.

There are rewards and punishments of behaviors, and they are at the whim of the instructor.

Managing classrooms versus controlling classrooms

Managing classrooms involves the following:

— creating a philosophy of teaching
— handling different situations in the classroom
— setting up space for learning, sharing, and listening
— organizing centers for learning (literature bulletin boards)
— placing teacher in the learning environment
— delivering creativity
— (teaching) giving directions that are clear and not multi-tiered
— managing time

— taking responsibility for learning among proactive students
— respecting the membership of individuals in the learning environment
— acknowledging belongingness to the learning environment through membership
— communicating and committing to self and others in the classroom through membership based on trust
— evolving teacher's role into facilitator/coach role
— allowing others input and differing of opinions, thoughts, and ideas through shared ownership of lessons
— being a positive role model (teacher, parent, student, administrator)
— leading by example
— paying attention to individual/student needs (managing each child's learning)
— getting results (i.e., testing, self esteem, self confidence)

On the other hand, controlling leadership behavior in the classroom promotes the following:

— Controlling by the leadership as forcing the learning environment to be from a one-sided perspective with little or no student input.
— Controlling is expecting from the teacher a parroting response from students with no creativity or nature response of the student.
— Controlling provides no opportunity for change.
— Controlling takes away individual and group identity.
— Involves thinking like the leader.
— Low or no creativity.
— No risks taken by students in their responses and learning.
— No or little opportunity to share others ideas.
— Submission to authority.
— Conforming to one or a limited ideology.

Various Teaching Techniques

There are various teaching techniques that can be demonstrated for successful teaching/learning in the classroom. Many of the techniques call for collaborations between teachers and students. It is imperative that individual learning styles be understood by the instructor. It is also important that different students learn differently in terms of content and information. It has been observed over the years that teachers tend to teach to their strengths. This in and of itself is not a negative thing, but when the student is not of the learning style of the teacher, then there is an adjustment that needs to be made, and usually, it is the student that is responsible for the adjusting in learning (Latham 1998, 104). Rules and learning also discloses one strategy is to view the rule-making experience.

Setting Rules with Students

What role do classroom rules play in effective instruction? If rules are primarily a means of maintaining discipline, then they relate to instruction only indirectly by contributing orderliness to the learning environment. Boostrom (1991) notes that a rules-as-discipline approach leads to a paradox. The rules may encourage passive acceptance instead of critical thinking and reflection in students. The solution, he argues, lies in thinking of rules not as being a means to an end, but as having direct implications for student learning. Schimmel (1997) and Blumenfeld-Jones (1996) echo this point. They argue that authoritative, patriarchal rule making by teachers is antithetical to the civic and social development of students in a democratic society.

Trusting students with the responsibility for shaping the rules will not lead to lax standards and nonexistent consequences; Castle and Rogers (1994) cite research showing that students frequently respond to such trust by developing rules that are strikingly similar to, and perhaps even stricter than, those advocated by their teachers. Thus allowing them and their parents to participate in the process does not so much affect what the rules look like as it does their perceptions of the rules. Students are far more likely to internalize and respect rules that they helped create than rules that are handed to them (Schimmel 1997).

Classroom Management and Student Assignments

Teachers give assignments in the course of teaching lessons. Assignments should be relevant to the lessons taught.

Assignments are usually given in two categories:

1. Long-range assignments
2. Short-range assignments

Long-range assignments can take a month, a semester, or entire year to complete. For long-range assignments, there should be dates assigned for completion of the projects and a check-in system for following students' progress with the long-range assignment(s). By having a check-in for the long-range assignment, you can better keep up with individual or group progress, dates of when segments are due, and time-management concerns that students may be experiencing while getting their work done.

Students and teachers alike must adhere to due dates. If due dates are not honored by the student, then consequences should established. At some point, the work not turned in on time cannot be accepted because of expectations—for completing assignments and student responsibility for getting their own work completed in a timely manner is part of lessons learned. All expectations need to be shared by the teacher at the beginning of the assignment and not addressed when there is an infraction.

Short-range assignments can be due in a day, week, biweekly, or a month. The purpose for short-range assignments is to check students' understanding of content taught on a daily basis. It is important that directions are clear and understood by the students as to what is required in the assignment. Will teachers establish a makeup—work policy, and how will it be enforced? Teacher time for grading papers and returning papers to students in a timely manner is equally important for several reasons. It is modeling behavior by the teacher that assignments are important enough to be returned so students can see their progress. Second, assignments many times can be used for test preparation. Third, assignments need to be spread out so that the teacher does not overwhelm him or herself with paperwork and get behind in grading papers. Fourth, setting deadlines and adhering to those deadlines so students can respect the importance of an assignment. Also, some assignments may need to be redone, and time management is quite important when redos are turned in and returned to students.

Teachers need to establish a reward-and-punishment system for assignments that are passed in on time, late, or no-show. This should all be done before assignments are given whether long-term or short-term assignments.

Homework is another important category for work to be completed. How much homework is given and for what purpose needs to be developed by the teacher before work is given. Students need to experience a relevancy for the work given. There needs to be a direct relationship from work done in class to homework given. It must be relevant, practical, and logical for the student. It cannot be busywork.

Assignments are a support and an extension of lessons taught. Assignments must be realistic for the student to make connections with learning information and prior knowledge.

CHAPTER TWO

Students: What They Want, Why They Need Self-Worth, Images of Self to Others, and Images of Self to Self

Most teachers are beginning to concern themselves with the self-worth of the children as well as the child's achievement . . . The ability to convey what a student has learned goes a long way toward building self-esteem. After all, shouldn't schools be in the business of training and preparing students to improve their abilities as well as believe that they get what they pay for?

—Gwin

I mages are all around us; and images bombard us in most of our experiences that we have with family, friends, opponents, collective groups, and individual pursuits. With images are combined messages that encourage, discourage, enrage, defuse, insight, alienate, entice, neglect, and enhance our experiences. Students, parents, teachers, and administrators try to emulate those images.

Self-Esteem Initiatives

Webster's Third New International Dictionary defines esteem as (1) confidence and satisfaction in oneself and (2) one's good opinion of oneself. If one accepts this definition, it then follows that a person or group of persons who lack self-esteem or—as is more likely—whose self-esteem is low will have a very difficult time coping in the real world. It also follows that a person or group with low self-esteem will be very susceptible to almost certain manipulation or control by others.

It also means that an individual or group of individuals seeking to control others will put much emphasis on breaking down their target's self-esteem (Bailey 1990, 13). There are two schools of thought concerning high self-esteem in children. Some psychologists believe that teaching high self-esteem will foster above-average academic achievement. Others believe that the demands of high academic achievement will positively affect self-esteem (Gwin 1990, 16).

The theory that a healthy self-concept can improve academic performance in the average child has contributed to the fact that most children have been taught some form of self-esteem. A number of theorists are now advocating that confidence boosting has a long and important tradition in the schools, but fear of failure and parental hovering have much more to do with success than good feelings about oneself. The self-esteem movement may be on a collision course with the growing movement to revive schools academically. Can this new self-esteem obsession ultimately undermine real education?

Various psychologists advocate that self-esteem happens when children really learn something. It grows when children are able to use what they have learned. This is a result of honest educational efforts. It is not a substitute for learning.

Most teachers are beginning to concern themselves with the self-worth of the children as well as the child's achievement. The ability to convey what a student has learned goes a long way toward building self-esteem.

After all, shouldn't schools be in the business of training and preparing students to improve their abilities as well as believe that they get what they pay for? (Gwin 1990, 16).

We certainly have not taught enough black boys and girls that self-respect is earned often with various difficulties. We have not instilled in enough of them the courage to excel twice as hard as they attempt to feel good. The fact remains that when children have high achievement, they usually feel good about themselves and usually display acceptable behavior.

The behavior of a child is often influenced by his/her perception. The mind is constantly accepting as well as filtering out various stimuli. One's aims, objectives, and moral disposition continuously influence one's perception. If we could get our youth to define and improve the definition of their perception, maybe they would be better able to clarify their attitudes, goals, and values.

Psychological studies of success and failure in our society reveal that one of the most important characteristics of successful people is accurate perception. It can then be reasoned that unrealistic perception leads to faulty judgment. Faulty judgment leads to unacceptable behavior; whereas, realistic perception leads to sound judgments. Sound judgment can easily lead to success. If a student does not have high self-esteem, it has to be taught. Self-esteem has to be taught either at home or away from home (Gwin 1990, 17-18).

Self-Esteem and Self-Worth

Self-esteem is important for all of us to experience. Self-esteem speaks directly to self-worth, self-appreciation, and self-like. There are five initial phrases that are presented, and the individual in the group must complete the phrases.

1. I am worth . . .
2. I value . . .
3. I protect . . .
4. I fear . . .
5. I know . . . and I respect . . .

The exercise can be done with kindergarten children as well as college students, parents, community people, and professional personnel. In the lower grades, the teacher can use magazines, pictures, and objects to demonstrate the six phrases. For example, "I value . . ."; a kindergartener or first grader may respond with "I value my mom, dad, pet." And a high school student may respond with "I value my car, job, money." No response is considered incorrect. The responses may be displayed in the room or written in a journal. The idea is to get children/students/participants to think about themselves in different ways. Teachers are advised not to give them the answers or to make value judgments. It is an information-sharing time. The question *why* can be asked after all have shared. The statements can be given one at a time over several weeks. The class may want to use the same statements and apply them to the entire group, e.g., "The entire class is worth . . ." Or "The class values . . ." The completed phrase may be shared in groups of two. This allows quiet sharing and trust building. If members of groupings want to share with the larger group, they are encouraged to do so.

Another exercise involves telling something really unique or "cool" about yourself. Tell about a hobby or activity that you are extremely good at doing. Someone else chooses someone and tells something positive about that person. Everyone must pick someone in the class until all are chosen. Write down the attributes on newsprint paper and display in the classroom. Find an object or item that best describes you as a person. Tell why you have chosen this item/object. Check with the class and see if anyone else agrees. If no one doesn't, that is quite all right. The choice is from the students' and teachers' perspective. The activities allow students to share and allow for freedom of expression to occur. No one in the class is permitted to be insulting or to be insulted by another person. The listeners are important to the speakers' presentations because the sharing helps the class learn more about the person speaking, and in turn, the listener can begin to receive understanding about class members as well as make connections with their own legacies. The individual sharing helps to build self-esteem and self-pride with one's own identity.

The purpose for the sharing and reflecting on information is so that each person can have center stage and talk to others about themselves. The foundations for building self-esteem, self-identity, and self-assurance are fostered by individual sharing. The sharing of information is a planned activity. Preparation by the teacher is primary in the success of the experience for the teacher and student.

Classroom Management with Models of Teaching

In the course, classroom management with models of teaching, validation of students is modeled in numerous ways. The following is an activity that my students have performed over the years. The question asked is for them to define "classroom management," working in small groups and sharing their findings. Each time, what is demonstrated is that students have a familiar idea of what classroom management is and it is not. It provides a platform for discussion and extended readings in class. It offers to students their participation for what I call "owning your own learning."

There is a discussion about what does "owning something" anything look and feel like to you. Name something you own. How do you treat what you own? Some responses included, What I own I

1. handle it with care,
2. take care of it,
3. value it,
4. take responsibility for it,
5. maintain it and watch over it,
6. respect it,
7. protect it.

The action words are then translated to the classroom environment and how does one own their own learning. What are the values in the classroom that effect all of the members of the classroom?

Graduate students have stated in their responses to the question, what is classroom management?

- It is structural provisions.
- It is student accountability.
- It is teacher accountability.
- It is creating a comfortable/safe environment that is conducive to learning.
- Students are active participants in all aspects of the classroom.
- It is flexibility (student/teacher discourse).
- It is classroom policies and expectations.
- It is student/parent-signed contract.
- It is open-door policy (feel welcomed).

Other concepts about classroom management include:

- Organization
- Cooperation (teamwork)
- Discipline
- Valuing yourself and students
- Clear and precise expectations (for students, teachers, parents, administrators)
- Knowing your students
- Positive classroom environment
- Students working to the best of their abilities
- Adhering to different learning styles
- Defined classroom rules
- Create an effective learning environment
- Have an incentive program
- Consistent behavior among student as well as teacher
- Everyone has a classroom job or responsibility
- Know the daily routine
- Know expectations
- Allowing and supporting meaningful dialogue to occur in the classroom

Using the KWL Method in Teaching

Students: What do they know, and how do they know it (what they know)? Using KWL in giving instruction is an effective way to find out what students know and begin the dialogue on from whom students know what they know. It is dividing a sheet of Post-it newsprint, whiteboard, power-point-presentation page into three columns—K/W/L.

K is what do you know about the given topic, theme, or subject to the lesson. W is what do you want to know? And L is what you have learned once the lesson has been implemented.

The KWL chart can be reviewed at any point of the lesson. It can be added to and used as a checkoff sheet for immediate information gathered and understood.

Preparation for teaching—involves planning, researching information, and implementing lessons—is essential. Lesson planning should include the following elements:

— title of lesson
— theme
— grade (ages and learning skills)
— goals (what you want to instruct)
— objectives (how you want to instruct—related to the goals and outcomes)
— procedure skills
— materials
— outcomes
— assessment(s)

A lesson plan (1) is a guide to instruction, (2) establishes your tasks, (3) provides students with direction, (4)allows the instructor to make notes and revisit lessons for connecting information and having follow-ups to a particular lesson. There are two questions paramount to lesson planning: What do you want students to know? And how do you access what students know?

There are a myriad of ways of knowing a particular kind of information. Herb Kohl (1998) states in his book *Discipline of Hope*. "If people don't discover things for themselves, they don't have true conviction, and the idea just disappears."

Jacqueline Jordan Irvine—an Emory University researcher and advocate for culturally responsive teaching—believes that "the challenge is to find better ways to connect to the realities of what students know and live." Irvine states, "Talk about race and race relations with students. It is part of their everyday lives." Culturally responsive teaching is not about one lesson on Dr. Martin Luther King Jr. during Black History Month. It is not serving tacos in the cafeteria on Cinco de Mayo. Beyond heroes and holidays, it is about understanding students' home life, their language, music, dress, behavior, ideas about success, the role of religion and community in their lives, and more. It is bringing the experiences of their twenty-four-hour day into the seven-hour school day to give them information in familiar context (Neatoday 2006, 28).

Consider your minority and low-income students' experiences as valuable tools, not deficits, says Denise Alston of NEA in Atlanta. It's called an assets-based model. And it means taking what others might discount as problems for a child poverty—English as a second language—and viewing them as building blocks for perseverance and resilience (Neatoday 2006, 30).

Students: What Empathy Can Do

Ernest Mendes states in his article "What Empathy Can Do" that students respond to us because we care and because they like us. Positive responses create an emotional bank account that can absorb relational difficulties that occur along the way. Earning the respect of students is not enough. Students must perceive that we care, and even that we like them deep down as people. In building relationships, students need both structure and nurture, and the ways in which the teacher responds to these needs in the classroom are crucial (59). Multiple intelligences begin for a variety of reasons; educators have regarded intelligence quotient (IQ) test scores with suspicion. Some claim that the tests are culturally bias, that motivation to perform well influences results (Siegler 1991). Let us conclude this section with discussing the intelligences and column left.

When we teach and assess in ways that respect different strengths, students learn and perform better. We can teach children to be intelligent in many ways and on many levels, and we can teach anything using any of Gardner's intelligences (ASCD 2006, 34).

Multiple intelligences theory was originally developed as an explanation of how the mind works—not as an education policy, let alone an education panacea. Adopting a multiple-intelligences approach can bring about a quiet revolution in the way students see themselves and others. Instead of defining themselves as either "smart" or "dumb," students can perceive themselves as potentially smart in a number of ways (ASCD 2006, 23).

The greatest potential of a multiple intelligences approach to education grows from the concept of a profile of intelligences. Each learner's intelligence profile consists of a combination of relative strengths and weaknesses among the different intelligences. Most people have jagged profiles, they process some types of information better than other types. Other students have a searchlight profile. They show less pronounced differences among intelligences.

Intelligences are not isolated; they can interact with one another in an individual to yield a variety of outcomes (ASCD 2006, 25).

Gardner's Nine Multiple Intelligences

Linguistic—It is the ability to understand and use spoken and written communication.

Logical-mathematical—It is the ability to understand and use logic and numerical symbols and operations.

Musical—It is the ability to understand and use such concepts as rhythm, pitch, melody, and harmony.

Spatial—It is the ability to orient and manipulate three-dimensional space.

Bodily-kinesthetic—It is the ability to coordinate physical movement.

Naturalistic—It is the ability to distinguish and categorize objects or phenomena in nature.

Interpersonal—It is the ability to understand and interact well with other people.

Intrapersonal—It is the ability to understand and use one's thoughts, feelings, preferences, and interests.

Existential—It is the ability to contemplate phenomena or questions beyond sensory data, such as the infinite and infinitesimal (Gardner 2006) and (ASCD 2006, 25). The multiple intelligences approach does not require a teacher to design a lesson in nine different ways so that all students can access the material. Rather, it involves creating rich experiences in which students with different intelligence profiles can interact with the materials and ideas using their particular combinations of strengths and weaknesses.

Often the experiences are collaborative. As the amount of information that student and adults must process continues to increase dramatically, collaboration enables students to learn more by tapping into others' strengths as well as into their own. In ideal multiple-intelligences instruction, rich experiences and collaboration provide a context for students to become aware of their own intelligence profiles to develop self-regulation and to participate more actively in their own learning (ASCD 2006, 27).

Building Active Learners

The multiple intelligences approach does not require a teacher to design a lesson in nine different ways so that all students can access the material. Rather, it involves creating rich experiences in which students with different intelligence profiles can interact with the materials and ideas using their particular combinations of strengths and weaknesses.

Often these experiences are collaborative. As the amount of information that students and adults must process continues to increase dramatically, collaboration enables students to learn more by tapping into others' strengths as well as into their own. In ideal multiple intelligences instruction, rich experiences and collaboration provide a context for students to become aware of their own intelligence profiles to develop self-regulation and to participate more actively in their own learning (ASCD 2006, 27).

Creating Sociograms for Studying Group Behaviors

Strategies for effective classroom management, creating sociograms, and studying behavior patterns of students and professionals in the classroom for more effective teaching and understanding of individuals and groups in the classroom are essential in understanding and working with various group dynamics in the learning environment. It involves language usage in conversations and observations of spoken and non-spoken language. The skills are needed to understand, translate, and decode the meaning of words, phrases, thoughts for sorting, connecting, and understanding ideas and thought patterns. Imaging pictures and word relationships, speech and language acquisition are important in decoding and communicating thoughts.

It is important for teachers to take notice of how students respond one to another in various groups in the classroom, lunchroom, playground, and after-school activities. What are the speech patterns used? In small group, who directs the conversation, and who participates in the dialogues? Does leadership for sharing information move around the group or remain with just one individual? Who listens and who responds to questions in the group? Who dominates the dialogue, and who appears to not share their ideas, thoughts, and opinions? Sociograms allow the observer-teacher to really get an honest read on what is happening in groups with communication networks. It has been revealed many times from the graduate students that who they thought was the leader was in fact not, and who they thought was the dominate communicator was in essence not. Sociograms provide the mechanism for true observations without interruptions. It is suggested that the observation time be fifteen to twenty minutes in length. Those being observed are given a symbol on a piece of paper. For the twenty minutes or less, show communication interactions of those in the observed group.

Three young female adults are having lunch. Two arrive together, having been talking to each other in the park across the street from the restaurant. They arrive at the restaurant and are seated. The third female joins them. She takes over the conversation and edges one out. A and B are seated and

C the late arrival takes over the conversation leaving A out of the dialogue. C and B talk with each other and A is isolated. For the observer, what really happened and how did the conversation determine the outcome? What other issues were at play in creating the outcome of isolation for one person? The observation exercise forces teachers, parents, onlookers to really pay attention to group dynamics, body language, nonverbal communication and individual agenda in interpersonal situations.

CHAPTER THREE

Teaching Content, Handling Discipline, and Growing As a Professional

The problem many schools have in teaching children to read, write, and think are, to a large extent, symptoms of the inequality that permeates our educational system. In fact, we would argue that unless our schools and classrooms are animated by broad visions of equity, democracy, and social justice, they will never be able to realize the widely proclaimed goal of raising educational achievement for all children the efforts to rethink our classrooms must be both visionary and practical. We can teach for the society we live in, or we can teach for the one we want to see.

—Rethinking Schools, Fall 2003

Teaching content and being able to access information for lesson planning are valuable in giving instruction. There are numerous sources for gathering information and creating creative plans for teaching in the classroom. There are textbooks, videos, conferences, DVD recordings, tapes, journals, articles, curriculum sources to mention a few options that provide a wide assortment of packages, education stores, museums, libraries, and internet content area—discipline-specific materials to be taught in the classroom.

Along with teaching content is having a clear handle on managing discipline (student-and-teacher behavior in the classroom). Discipline for students in the classroom is a serious matter that influences classroom flow with activities and individual/group responsibility for demonstrating cooperation and respect. Students must have a level of agreement for their behavior on the classroom. There is a point when listening, paying attention, and clearly not talking on the students' part is required to receive information, directions, outcomes, and next steps expected in the instruction. These are paramount for the implementation of the lesson.

Lesson Planning

Planning lessons and keeping in mind the age appropriate with goals and objectives for activities are important in unit planning. Understanding the differences between goals and objectives really clarifies the purpose for lesson planning. Goals are the what of the lesson. What do you want to teach? Objectives are the how of the lesson. How will the objectives support the goals established for the lesson? Do we understand the concept of lesson outcomes and their relationship to goals and objectives. Lesson planning is having a clear point of what the lesson is inspired to give concretely what is to be learned and how are questions formulated. The outcomes address this concern.

Each lesson needs an outcomes reality. I maintain that you must have an idea of what the conclusion of the lesson holds for students. With outcomes clearly defined, then goals and objectives can be created for the lesson to be taught. There is a direct correlation between outcomes and goals and objectives. One supports the other in lesson implementation.

Case in point: If I am teaching a lesson about the parts of a plant, my outcomes for the lesson have to be clearly stated before I even begin planning the goals and objectives for the lesson. I ask myself the following questions: Where do I want students to be, and what do I want them to know when the lesson is completed? What is my wish list for the end of the lesson? The goals (the what of the lesson I am teaching), the objectives (the how I am teaching that supports the goals), materials, and activities are related to the outcomes of the lesson before the lesson is even taught. Once the lesson is completed, how do my outcomes measure up to what I was expecting from the lesson? Did my goals and objectives support the teaching style and materials used? What were the students' responses to the activities given? What did I learn from the experience of teaching about plants? What do I need to change for next time, and what/how do students connect this lesson to other lessons and other ideologies related or not related to plants? What is the KWL: What do the students already know? What do the students want to know? And When is the lesson completed, or what have the students learned?

A Caring and Supportive Teacher

Being a caring and supportive teacher does not mean coddling; rather, it means holding students accountable while providing the support they need to succeed. Research on adolescents finds that students in this age group define caring teachers as those who communicate directly and regularly with them about their academic progress and make sure they understand what has been taught (Wentzel 2006, 47). The key to raising achievement is connecting students with teachers who support them not only as learners but also as people (ASCD 2006, 47).

The spotlight on performance created by NCLB (No Child Left Behind) and other accountability policies must not distract us from attending to factors that substantially affect how well student perform. The most difficult-to-reach students will often goal out for a teacher who demonstrates caring for them as individuals and commitment to their success. School policies that support positive relationships between teachers and students can contribute significantly, not only to students' social-emotional health and well-being, but also to their academic performance. That's why paying attention to students' nonacademic needs is a key ingredient in schools' efforts to meet today's high-academic expectations (Stipek 2006, 49).

What Students Want When Asked

What students have said about what they wanted from teachers were taken from *the Rigor Retreat* in January 12, 2006, from *Looking at the*

Student Perspective: Research room the Minority Student Achievement Project From the text Fires in the Bathroom.

Re: Fostering Positive Classroom Behavior
Let us know your plan for the class.
Work with us on expectations for classroom behavior.
Follow up promptly and consistently on the agreed-upon expectations.
When trouble occurs, keep an open mind and establish the facts.
Make time to listen to us.

Re: How to Show Respect, Trust, and Fairness
Let us know what to expect from you and from the class.
Push us to do our best and push us equally.
Grade us fairly.
Keep your biases to yourself.

Re: Creating Success
Make clear your criteria for assessing our performance.
Offer good models and help us see why they are good—not just their faults.
Give helpful feedback and expect us to revise.
Remind us often that you expect our best.
Don't favor the students you think will do the best.

CHAPTER FOUR

Parents, Grandparents, Guardians and Teachers Alike Need to Reach Out One to the Other

Children have never been good at listening to their elders, but they have never failed to imitate them.

—James Baldwin

There must be a relationship with the teacher, paraprofessional, staff, counselor, principal, and other key administrator in the learning environment. I maintain and believe you cannot teach totally effectively without the support and involvements of parents/guardians. Teaching is not a solo journey. It is collaboration between school and home. The parents/guardians are intricate parts of the equation in the learning environment. The outreach for teachers to parents is nonnegotiable and vice versa. It can occur in many forms. Teachers and parents can use newsletters, classroom correspondence, telephone, e-mail, direct visitation to social setting, religious place of worship, community setting, home visit (applicable), open houses, and conferences. It is vitally important to understand that parents/guardians have various working hours and, in many cases, more than one place of employment. There are parents/guardians who may be unemployed and yet unavailable for contact. Each situation is different. Teachers and parents must form collaborations to interface and support each other. There must be dialogue and an ongoing communication system put in place and maintained by both teacher and parent.

Another major concern for parent/guardian communications may be that many children are homeless and live in shelters, hotel rooms, cars, and literally on the street. This living situation is challenging and devastating for the family at-large and the child in particular. Homelessness effects a high percentage of children in a myriad of ways. Temporary housing and sometimes moving from school to school can lend itself to insecurity and low self-esteem issues. Keeping up with expected school assignments and having the full resources to accomplish tasks are sometimes not possible.

In many instances, parents are not the only adults raising children or adolescence. Sometimes there are stepparents, older siblings, aunts, uncles, or cousins in the guardian role. Grandparents have become a vital part in many children's lives. They are raising their children's children.

Parents, guardians, and child advocates are in the midst of raising children in a world that they are not always familiar with themselves. Adults tend to rely on how they were raised and disciplined by their parents and guardians.

So what do parents/guardians do, say, know, believe, think, pray for regarding their children and themselves? There are as many answers as there are parents and families.

A Parent Forum

I co-lead a parent group at my place of worship. The need for the parent forum came about because parents voiced their concern for having a forum to talk, share, learn, get, and give support and have a space and place to be parents helping themselves and other parents in their adult walk on a daily basis. The group meets once a month and has been an inspiration and uplifting place for parents to be reaffirmed and supported in a positive manner.

Four questions are at the heart of the matter:

1. How is my language/tone perceived by my child or children?
2. Is there respect for my role and authority in the family? (How do my children experience my attitude toward their behaviors?)
3. Do I intently listen to my children on a daily basis?

It is imperative that parents be conscious about their effect of language and attitude when directly speaking and listening to their children. Parents are truly concerned with what happens to and with their children. Parents are competing with the world at-large. It is daunting for many parents with all of the external variables that directly impact their child's life. Parenting is challenging, all consuming, and downright difficult at times. Many parents/guardians are raising children by themselves on a daily basis. This situation adds anxiety, frustration, and aloneness to the parenting role.

Attitude is an important facet in our lives at home, in school, and on the job. To raise positive kids, according to Zig Ziglar, you must understand that to provide ongoing motivation for yourself and the kids, you need to receive motivational input on a regular basis. With the positive input on a steady basis, you will automatically seek out and apply the positive approach to life's daily challenges (Ziglar 2002, 48-49).

Three Stages in Childhood

Raising positive kids is not easy (Ziglar 2002, 52). The early years of childhood are the prime years in the child's moral development. He/she needs to know what he/she ought to do before he/she can think or put into practice what should be done. This learning begins at birth and will be taught primarily by those closest to him/her. There will never be a better time to teach obedience, which is the first element in the development of the conscience and moral sense.

During these early years, the child lives in a world of feeling and discovery rather than reason. The physical touch, the emotional climate, the tone of voice, and the atmosphere of the family in general are felt very early. But the child is not helped by trying to reason with him/her. He/she is dependent upon parents for direction. They need rules to follow. The small child becomes confused if made to reason and decide his/her own conduct (Ziglar 2002, 58).

The second age of childhood is the age of imitation, which occurs between the ages of eight and twelve. This is the period of time when as John Balguy says, "Whatever parents give their child good instruction and set them at the same time a bad example, may be considered as bringing them food in one hand and poison in the other." During these years, role models are most important to a child. Rules are important, but example is a great stimulus (58).

The next stage is the age of inspiration—ages thirteen and up. During the teenage period, the child is inspired by great ideas of one kind or another. They must have heroes. If they are not given heroes, they will find them; if they are not inspired by the right kind of heroes, they will be inspired by the wrong kind. During this period, a great deal of stability and character is gained if the teenager has a certain goal in mind. They need both short-range and long-range goals. Rules and limits are, of course, still important. By now, however, the adolescent needs to have inner controls to be effective because their parents cannot possibly be present at all times. The teenager needs to bring all past experiences to bear.

By the time a child becomes an adolescent, they know exactly what their parents believe. They do not always comprehend the reasons behind the beliefs. That is why it is so important to take time to communicate to your children why you believe what you believe. Standards and beliefs are reinforced by conversation: the youth needs to hear themselves and their parents as well as peer talk about the important aspects of life. Above all during the adolescent stage, the child needs to feel the love, confidence, and support of the parents. When acceptance and love come through, the adolescent will also be open to all kinds of changes for the good (Ziglar 2002, 60).

The three ages of childhood provide different approaches to child-rearing and child support. With each age of childhood, there are expectations and rewards for both the child and the parent. There are a host of factors that contribute to the stages of childhood development.

There is the home factor of role and responsibility for each of the family members. There is the cultural differences/similarities that exist for each of the families of color. There is the religious value and belief system that is in place.

There is the financial factor of earning money and spending patterns. There is the expectation for achievement and success that parents want for their children. There is the skill, intelligence, and special-needs factors that children possess. There is the social and class factors that influence what families are able to overcome. There is the age factor of parents and guardians that influence a value system in and out of the home. There are family-member relationships that weigh heavily on communications and getting along one with the other.

Simply Put: Parenting—It Is Never Done

This pronouncement sounds unrealistic to many because many of us have set a preconditioned time for when our parenting is completed. Some say early teens of their children while others say eighteen years of age. Still others say that once the child has completed undergraduate or professional trade school, and then there are a few who hold out for completion of graduate school. Whatever time frame you have chosen to be finished parenting, perish the thought. Parenting is a continuous relationship and commitment that last a lifetime. Different stages of a child's development require different parenting skills and objectives.

Parenting and teaching are so closely related in outcomes, goals, and objectives for students and adults alike. Attached is a working list or rules for possible improved parenting skills to assist in communicating and making informed decisions with children and adults as well. They include the following:

1. Abandon fixed ideas.
2. Think of ways to make it possible.
3. Go for the simple solution, not the perfect one.
4. Correct mistakes right away.
5. Use your wits, not your wallet.
6. Problems are opportunities.

7. Repeat why? five times.
8. No excuses needed.
9. Seek ideas from many people.
10. There is no end to improvement.

Parents and "Me" Time in Mind

Parents need and must find and take time for "me" time. It may be twenty minutes in each week. It may be honed to three hours in a month just for you. This time is to be reflective—have some pampering done, go shopping, or just window-shopping (without the children or mate). You may have a girlfriend and, if male, a male-friend "moment" to enjoy each other's company. Just talking, laughing, crying, sharing, and reaffirming self are vitally important. Setting the agenda for the family meetings should be shared by all involved in the meeting.

There should be an appointed time for the meetings, and the meeting should be created like an appointment for the family members to meet. The family meeting should be posted with reminders verbally given from time to time.

Another concern in parents and "me" time is chores for children and family members need to be public information. Chores need to be adhered to, and there should be no surprises or denying whose time it is to do a particular chore. Chores should be rotated.

As parents, there is a need to reduce the number of times you make a request for something to be done. Get down to saying or asking something once or twice at the most. Time is important. Make eye contact when making the requests as much as possible. Yelling through the house is not the answer. Do not chase children around to get them to stop and pay attention. As the parent, you stand in one place and request they come where you are. If not, go to where they are and do not run around. Be firm, yet caring.

There are those times when primal screams are in order. It is not a daily occurrence. It is usually a last resort of being exasperated and clearly down to your last "good" nerve and losing it. Primal screams should be explained ever so briefly and move on with what you were doing.

A key point for parents in disciplining children is that it is the child's behavior, not their persons that you are not pleased with. This is a difficult concept for parents to conceive, i.e., as a parent I do not like what you did or said—I like you, not your attitude. It is important to separate the two realities one from the other. When children hear and know that you do not like what they have done, they translate it into that you do not like them. This for the most part is not true. Over time that can build up on the child that there is a severe dislike for them, and they internalize your language to mean that who they are is problematic but just their behavior.

There are a host of situations that parents and children find themselves in as each is exploring the other. Children want regardless of what they articulate—boundaries set and adhered to—to know that someone is clearly in charge, that no is no and not maybe, that your value system as a parent means something to you and therefore to them, and that you want respect as they do. Children will ask for material items because they can, and it is your responsibility to not always comply with their requests. Some things are earned and worked for, and some things are not granted because they are unrealistic for the child to have.

It is my belief that students want to be respected, felt and be valued about who they are, treated fairly and honestly, and acknowledged as having a valued membership in the classroom, individual family, and school community. Validation goes a long way in accepting a person/student. Communicating (talking and listening) to ideas and ideologies by using active listening skills are ways of setting up validation assurances for students. Active listening is concentrating on what is said or asked. It is repeating to the person what you have heard, asked, or stated. It is finding clarity of language and meaning. It is questioning or stating what was said to you. It is not judging or being condescending one to another. This form of dialogue helps to validate the speaker and the listener as well. It provides wait time for thinking about a response before speaking. It may be difficult at first to use this way of communicating, but eventually if given time, it will assist you in redirecting your first impulses to speak or fire back without knowing for sure if you are really responding to what was asked or said. It takes practice, and it takes time.

Parenting is a lifelong journey and commitment. It changes, and it redefines itself depending on the age of the child/children. It does not go away or take a vacation. It is my resolve that parenting is the most important and valuable task given to me and us. There are no guarantees, yet there is everlasting prayer and faith that gets you through the various stages of childhood growth and development. For me, it is a faith walk that includes tears, joy, sadness, happiness, anger, loss, change, setting boundaries, modeling behaviors, saying no and meaning it, letting go, building trust, learning patience, praying, and giving continuous love.

Parenting is by any stretch of the imagination not easy, but not impossible. There are moments of extreme joy and unspeakable fear depending upon the given situation parents and children find themselves living. There are no guaranteed answers to questions. There is one certainty—children evolve in spite of us or maybe because of us. It is a journey in my mind's eye so worth taking.

The following is a shared discussion of the parents meeting in May 2007:
Roberta Green has been an engaging parent and gracious notetaker in all of our meetings and recaps the essence of our discussions.

— We talked about the importance of our children and ourselves having a true understanding of racism.
— We talked about our children being appreciative of what they have and the importance of them understanding poverty.
— We talked about God being in the mix of all things in our lives.
— We talked about how we as parents should consistently sit down and talk to our children about current events. These topics should include social issues, economics issues, and racist issues. It was suggested that consistently would be done once a week.
— We talked about how do we help our children to deal with the "unknown" around race and culture, and how do we help them to pick their battles.
— We talked how having the hard conversations (race) can be painful as it causes us to look at ourselves and things that might have happened to us.
— We talked about acknowledging our children.
— We talked about power and how that plays into one having the ability to be racist.
— We talked about the fact that people of color can act racist, but can't be racist as they don't have power. Remember or be informed that racism is based on the system of those with established power.

An Overview of Our April 2007 Meeting

Hello, Roberta and Parent Group,

1. Adoptive children have a different journey in life, and the issues of abandonment and trust really influence how decisions get made by

them in real-life situations. There are lingering questions that these children have about being wanted and cared for in a supportive family.

2. Young people dealing with trusting adults in power positions/ positions of authority and when the adult role is compromised by poor judgment, rudeness, gender insensitivity, bigotry, and racism. Giving children the skills they need to make effective choices when confronted by negative behavior in adults and teaching children to trust their "gut instincts" and what that really means.

3. Giving children the gift of prayer and scripture reading that can support them in troubling situations.

The meeting on the 27th of April was truly a blessing.

As parents, you are doing an awesome task of raising your children and others' children as well.

With all that occurs in our lives, God must be in the mix. No doubt, no question about this. God Bless you all. Ethlyn

May 2007 Meeting Discussions

Good day all.

Just a reminder that we will be meeting this Friday, May 4 at 6:00 pm at the Church.

Our last meeting (April 27, 2007) was a blessing.

It was filled with support and compassion. Below is a brief recap of the sharing:

— Sharing about our family meetings. One mom shared that during their family meetings they plan their meals for the week.
— Talked about how do we help our children to trust their instincts, and how do we know what bothers them. We were instructed to pose the question to them.
— Talked about the importance of children having a clear understanding of what we won't tolerate.
— We must understand that our children may make us cry at times.
— We must understand that at times we need to select when to speak to our children.
— There is no exact cookie cutter that was branded for raising children.
— Oh yes, controlling behaviors were discuss. Yes controlling behaviors by some of us parents.

— Then there was my favorite, the wonderful world of adolescence.
— We were reminded/informed that adolescence is the age of inspiration.
— There was sharing about how it is still important for adolescents to have rules and limits. It is the rules and limits that help our children to gain inner controls that are effective. This is a much needed tool, as we as parents can not always be there.
— The final word on this was communicate. Communicate with your children and listen carefully to what is said by them and you.
— There was sharing around those moments/struggles with our children, and the fact that it is okay for our children to see us pray in the midst of the moment.
— Talked about how some of the things that our teens go through will open up reflections for us as parents.
— Lastly, that at times we may need to stop the behaviors/actions of our children and ask them what they want.
— Adoptive children have a different journey and there are issuesof abandonment and trust. (Remember all of the above helps to build their character and get them ready for being in the world. Also trusting adults in power positions when the role is comprised by poor judgment, rudeness, gender, insensitivity and bigotry. The parents were given a homework assignment after the session that supported the meeting agenda.

The parent forum meetings have become a place for parents to talk, share, cry, laugh, reaffirm, question, support and provide assurances for each other in their daily walk. There is always a potluck supper prepared and served by the parents. Eating and talking at this fellowship table enhances the dialogue and friendships that occur in this setting.

CHAPTER FIVE

Teaching Styles and Cultural Diversity

The models of teaching are Social Family, Personal Family, Informational Family and Behavioral Family. Each of these families describes a manner for teaching and providing instruction in teaching content and focusing on multicultural diversity information.

In the classroom, a model of teaching creates a certain social system within the classroom, and this social system is learned as well. Properly implemented models based on democratic process create a democratic social system and require students to learn the skills of negotiation. Those emphasizing competition provide competitive social systems that are experienced and learned by students. Method defines the emphasis given to content, provides a process to be learned, and provides a social climate that will greatly influence the behavior of learners toward one another and toward the teacher. The effects of the method are complex and multidimensional (Joyce and Weil 1986, 403).

There are four families of teaching models: the behavioral family (drawing particularly on the work of B. F. Skinner, many models have been designed to take advantage of the human being's capacity to learn and modify behavior by responding to tasks and feedback), the social family (these models create education by confronting students with problems that they must solve together, by leading students to analyze their values and the public policies that shape justice in or society, and by introducing students to increasing their social skills and understanding), the personal family (all learning ultimately depends on the focused education of the individual student and has its expression in the enhancement of the self and support of one another's struggles to achieve meaning and strength for self-responsible self-determination), and the informational family (to educate students and influence their information process and specifically to help students acquire and operate on data) (Joyce and Weil, iv-vi: 24).

Inclusive in the four families are ten models of teaching. The ten models are nondirective teaching, group investigation, synectics, gestalt (awareness oriented), advance organizer, inductive thinking, inquiry training, cybernetic simulation, cybernetic training, and behavior modification (Joyce and Weil 1986, 417).

The ten models of teaching provide ten probable outcomes. They are 1.self-understanding, 2. awareness, 3. creativity,4. interpersonal skills,5. social values, 6.academic inquiry, 7, concepts, 8, factual material, 9, academic skills, and

10. psychomotor skills (Joyce and Weil, 417). The outcomes of the teaching models effect the level of student learning and development of self-esteem and achievement in a learning environment. The outcomes of the teaching models effect the level of student environment.

Behaviors and Learning

There are real differences among the approaches to teaching, and these differences affect what is learned. Essentially, teaching is the creation of learning environments, and different environments are directed toward and nurture different kinds of learning. Hunt's reformulation of Lewin's maxim that if behavior is a function of a person/environment, then selected learning experiences are essentially a coordination of objectives, learner, and environment (Joyce and Weil 418). Teaching cultural diversity to a diverse classroom population should incorporate the ten models of teaching. Specifically, the approaches to teaching having an effect on how cultural diversity is introduced and taught in the learning environment permits the teacher and student to learn from each other.

Education is a matter of purpose and focus. To educate a child is to act with the purpose of influencing the child's development as a whole person. What you do may vary. You may teach him/her, you may play with him/her, you may structure his/her environment, you may censor television, or you may pass laws to keep him or her out of bars. But you may not do any of these things for purposes other than to educate the child. That is why you cannot just peek in on someone and tell whether or not he or she is engaged in education. You have to watch him/her for some time and perhaps even question him/her to see what they are up to in their teaching (Bereiter, 1973, 6)

Teaching well involves the skill and ingenuity to reconstruct the curriculum, redesign the environment, and change one's own behavior so that one's students will have the experiences, resources, and support they need to develop their sensitivity, compassion, and intelligence (Kohl 1998, 30). What we reveal about ourselves, the curriculum we select for our classroom, and the way we structure classroom interactions can send powerful messages to students about their own self-worth and sense of belonging in the educational process (Challenges for the Classroom, Facing History and Ourselves News, 1990).

Similarly, teachers also observe students, ask questions, and make judgments about work habits, information from lessons taught, classroom behavior, interpersonal relationships that are observed. Communication plays an important role in teacher/student interactions in the classroom. How does the teacher begin to share about him/herself in the classroom about cultural diversity?

There are many behaviors and attitudes that teachers have, which disclose to children who they are but not always why they are a certain way. Those behaviors and attitudes are observed by children every day when there is an interface with teachers. The way teachers walk into a room, how a teacher starts a lesson, where a teacher walks in the room during the lesson, how and where a teacher sits or stands in the room when activities are taking pile, and the kind of voice a teacher uses to give directions or get a response from a child are referred to as a style of behavior in a learning/teaching environment. Students are quick to learn what each teacher's style and responses are in order that they will know how to behave or not behave for a particular teacher in a given classroom situation. Student behaviors and classroom situations introduce the importance of classroom management as it relates to cultural diversity. Teacher behaviors in the classroom influence student learning, student self-esteem, learning outcomes, and teacher effectiveness.

Teacher Behaviors and Attitudes

There are also real differences in teacher behaviors and teacher attitudes regarding curriculum, student learning styles, student achievement, teacher effectiveness, and teacher competency. It is the behaviors and attitudes of individuals and groups in various learning settings whether preschool, kindergarten through grades twelve, or undergraduate/graduate school. It is crucial to take time in the beginning of introducing cultural diversity in the classroom to set a teaching and learning atmosphere of trust, tolerance or ambiguity, patience with emotional differences, and support as to take time at the end of the experience to reflect with the class on what it was like for each person in the class. Teaching cultural diversity in the classroom encourages students and teachers to experience a legacy of self. Cultural diversity is the sharing by individuals (students and teachers) of their ethnic heritage and legacy with the class or seminar. In the classroom setting, each individual is encouraged to share something or someone related to their family with the class/group. It is important to listen to our own histories and acknowledge others' histories as we learn about diversity and ourselves in the learning environment.

A Teacher's Responsibility-Learning about our own biases and prejudices

The teaching/learning environment has provided a potpourri of experiences that continue to challenge the adult learner and teacher. To assist teachers with their issues concerning stereotypes, prejudices, and biases either realized or imagined is an ongoing process for teachers' growth and development in education.

One of several missions I have chosen in teaching is helping teachers to own their own cultural diverse perceptions. I believe teachers have a responsibility to foster nonjudgmental and non-prejudicial behavior toward their students. It is not enough to be thoroughly prepared to teach in the classroom, but one must be informed, sensitive, and responsive to ethnic/cultural issues for themselves and the students they teach.

It has been my approach in teaching cultural diversity issues to never ask teachers or students if teachers have prejudices or biases, but rather make the definitive statement that teachers being people are biased and prejudiced. This allows for there not to be a long discourse of denial and defensiveness on the educators' part in course discussions. More importantly, how do educators deal with land, manage their prejudices and biases in the classroom, and live in the larger society?

To answer this and other related questions about biases and prejudices, I have created a questionnaire for graduate students who have tackled questions/responses in the class. Some of the responses are shared in this chapter. The responses are revealing and create a starting point for educators to examine their effective teaching/training skills side by side with their own acknowledged prejudices and biases.

1. What is stereotype in your own definition?
2. Are there differences in stereotypes among members of the same ethnic groups and between ethnic groups?
3. Are there any lessons learned from your own experience with prejudices/biases and stereotypes? Discuss.
4. How do stereotypes foster prejudices/biases and vice versa? Discuss.

Beyond the questions are answers and a newfound reality about teaching and learning that can make a difference for the teacher. Teachers are able to define stereotypes for themselves. Second, they can name their own stereotypes and can adopt a behavior that they exhibit toward the stereotype. Teachers can actively choose which stereotypes they want to work on getting rid of and why. They share their lessons learned and keep a working journal to reflect what their experiences are on a daily/weekly basis. In many instances, teachers choose different groups to belong to in their schools and hold their friends more accountable for their beliefs and comments.

Two Different Teaching Arenas

I have taught in several teaching arenas over the years. One arena involves graduate students who teach in urban and suburban classrooms. The second arena involves undergraduate students who are beginning their teaching careers. They student teach in mostly urban settings. Both groups of students approach teaching differently because each group is at a different stage of teaching.

I am not comparing responses to looking at cultural diversity, but rather what is the approach to learning about individual stereotypes and prejudices that are carried into the classroom by teachers at different stages of teaching.

For the undergraduate students, the approach to teaching cultural diversity starts with students identifying in their practicum classrooms the students' ethnic and cultural backgrounds. Once the ethnic backgrounds are confirmed by the students, then the student teachers must do research on the ethnic backgrounds. In seminar class, student teachers are asked to first guess what they think their students' ethnic backgrounds are. They then share what they know about what they have guessed. This shows how much they may or may not know. Student teachers then prepare a questionnaire to find out what each of them knows about their ethnic group and culture. This has been quite revealing. Most of the students were incorrect about their initial observations.

In seminar class discussions, there are focused questions asked during the course of the semester. These questions serve as the framework for dialogue in seminar discussions.

1. What does the old information reveal about your understanding about ethnic groups?

2. How does what you know influence how you teach students?
3. Are there embedded in your knowledge base stereotypes and prejudices that are unfounded?
4. What do you do with the new information that you find out about your students?
5. How do you increase your knowledge base about ethnicity and culture?
6. How do you incorporate your own ethnic knowledge into teaching students who are from the same or different ethnic groups as your own?

The student teachers must also do their own ethnic background search and share in the seminar class. Each student must also bring in a symbol that represents them and their ethnic group. This is an oral presentation in class, and peers are encouraged to ask questions and make comments.

The activity has proven insightful and beneficial for many of the students in the class. They are learning about their own ethnicities and the possible stereotypes, biases, and prejudices that are projected in their own ethnic group. They direct questions and observations that they have made and also ask for peer feedback. Many for the first time are taking a serious look at their own identities and what that means to them. Sometimes there is laughter, and sometimes there is sheer amazement about what is not understood or known about culture and ethnic information.

The conversations and observations create a shift in student thinking. The seminar makes student teachers realize that their students are multidimensional. They have histories, culture, and interests that transcend the classroom. Some of the student responses have been the following:

Now I know more about my students' backgrounds.
I am beginning to know more about my own history and legacy that
    I did not know before.

There is a lot to know and still teach in the classroom.
I have to be careful not to put everybody in the same ethnic group
    from now on as I teach.

I just didn't know stuff.
Nobody ever told us in school about culture and history.
I have to think more when I choose materials to teach.
Wow, teaching is really hard work.

Students in the practicum seminar are encouraged to continue their research on ethnicity and culture. Each week, they are asked to reflect in their journals about their biases, prejudices, and stereotypes about people and ideas. All of this new information is overwhelming for some students. I encourage the students to deal with what is manageable at the moment. You cannot take it all on at once. For starters, just be informed and aware of your behaviors/attitudes toward students and ideas that are different to you. Try not to be defensive. Try to defer judgments. Working with a consciousness about culture and ethnicity is an ongoing process. It is not completely learned in a day, week, or year. It is a lifetime pursuit. Reading, asking questions, making discoveries about yourself and others, and making changes in how you relate to others are all part of the teaching/learning work we do in and out of the classroom.

In the graduate course on cultural diversity in the workplace, the students are mostly teachers. In class, they are asked about their fears, values, and knowledge. There is a course activity that I have graduate students participate in that help them and me to begin the dialogue about biases, prejudices, and stereotypes. I ask students to write on a sheet of paper three handles (beginning phrases) and give as many responses to each handle as they can think of in five to six minutes. The handles are "I value . . ." "I fear . . ." "I know . . ." It is at first glance an easy exercise. But once done, students respond "This is not as easy as it looks." It really causes one to be reflective and take time to think and write. There is a sharing with others in the group after the exercise is individually completed. Ultimately, the sharing in group leads to discussions about family, inhibitions, likes/dislikes, and a myriad of thoughts/ideas about their realities and belief systems.

Teaching cultural diversity and ownership for reactions/actions— coupled with reading, writing, and thinking—does permit teachers and professionals in a supportive learning environment to share, question, and, in many cases, begin to resolve some "long and safe" notions about biases, prejudices, and stereotypes. This is an ongoing process of disclosure. Talking, listening, sharing, reading, writing, and thinking lead to one's own responsibility for addressing issues about identity, self-worth, and the attitudes of people in various situations. Students are asked to share their ethnic legacies and the historical importance they hold for them as professionals.

More specifically, I ask direct questions to my students about who they are, who they perceive themselves to be, and who they see their students being from an ethnic-cultural perspective in the classroom. It is one thing to teach about cultural diversity and teach diverse students and quite another to look at one's own perceptions about cultural diversity, stereotypes, biases, and prejudices. To further extend this notion of cultural diversity to include individual feelings and experiences about diversity really challenges one's own value system and belief system. It calls into question one's own shortcomings in dealing with students who are the same or different from the teacher socially, ethnically, racially, religiously, and culturally.

It is first important to know what the teacher's prejudices and biases are. Are the biases and prejudices "people related" or ideology? List those prejudices and, next to each one, ask, when did they first occur in your life as you remember? Second, ask, why do these prejudices work for you? How are they comfortable for you to have them? Third, choose one or two to really work on that you want to be rid of in your life. How does one do that?

Acknowledging your feelings and discomfort with your prejudices and biases is important to note. Listen to the messages you constantly send yourself in specific situations. Acknowledge what you are really afraid of when certain things happen concerning people and their responses to you. Choose a new behavior to experience when confronting your biases and prejudices.

Ask yourself, what must I do differently? How am I responding to communicating or behaving toward an idea or person? What am I allowing to happen and not responding to in any way? Do I just accept situations and do not take the time to say, Wait a minute, what do you mean, or what did you really say? There is a personal responsibility to ask questions of yourself and others around you. Do I listen and respond in a manner that permits me to question my assumptions? A colleague of mine says frequently, "Do not assume, it could be otherwise." The statement is truer than one would believe.

This Is Not Easy to Talk About and Share

This is never easy to talk about and share, but it is necessary in order to be more open and less judgmental in and out of the classroom. Yes, teachers in general are nurturers and protectors, as well as builders of children's self-identity and self-esteem. What must teachers know about their self-esteem and self-identity? It is critically important for teachers to acknowledge to themselves and others their self-esteem issues. Why, because if we are responsible for nurturing and building student self-esteem and self-identity, there is a responsibility for teachers to find a comfort level that gives them self-affirmation.

I firmly believe you cannot give someone something that you do not possess. In other words, if you do not have self-esteem, you cannot assist others in acquiring it. It begins for teachers with acknowledgement for the things we do well in and out of the classroom. It has to do with how we put ourselves down on a constant basis. It has to do with changing our relationship with ourselves to value ourselves in what we do and how we teach.

I have come to terms in many ways with my own biases, prejudices, and stereotypes. I have faced what is uncomfortable for me about others' attitudes and dealt with prejudices toward me by peers and students. Grappling with my misgivings about racial differences/similarities and confronting those feelings of mistrust have allowed me to be honest about what I see and know. There is sometimes rage about specific situations and how decisions are made by others in the world around me. In my professional world, choosing team members and working with people and students who do not have a similar value system is challenging in and of itself.

What do I value and why? The answer is in my past and also in my present. The answer is about change in thinking, processing, believing, taking risks, and trying to be nonjudgmental about various situations and people. As with my undergraduate practicum students, they are on a mission to find out who their students are. They are also on a mission to find who they are from an ethnic-cultural perspective. They are reading, writing, and asking questions about people and themselves. My graduate students are sharing ethnicities and reaffirming who they are as people.

Who Are You, and Who Are You Teaching in the Classroom?

The question, Who are you, and who are you teaching in the classroom? arises from my supervising students during their practicum semester. In a seminar class that meets once a week, students are asked to share their daily routines, interactions with students in their practicum setting, lessons planned and taught.

Discussions students have with their cooperating teachers during the day and week are also shared in class. Each student is responsible for keeping a written journal of activities and reflections. The journal is checked twice during the semester. The journal is part of a final seminar assignment collected at the end of the semester.

The seminar by design addresses the students teaching in the classroom. The students in the seminar class are undergraduate students. Their backgrounds vary, and their reasons for becoming teachers vary as well. Some have wanted to become teachers for a long time. Others have been influenced by their own teachers and realized a need to become teachers. Each of the students has practicum in urban settings with the exception of four students who teach in a suburban setting.

Beginning this particular semester, I was faced with seven of nine students that I previously taught in a method of teaching course. A little background is important now. In the previously taught methods course, there were rigorous assignments and one in particular that got the students' attention. The assignment had to do with each student doing an impromptu lesson from a subject that I gave to them to teach at a moment's notice.

The activity of impromptu teaching was new and frightening for many of the students. They expressed being scared to teach in front of their peers. They expressed being scared in not knowing ahead of time what the subject would be that they had to teach. They expressed panic and discomfort at getting the teaching right in front of their peers the first time. They did not want to be embarrassed or critiqued for their teaching. With all of this reluctance and fear, the assignment was not negotiated. There were class discussions about preparedness for student teaching. There were discussions about what do you know and how do you know certain information. There were discussions about being asked to stand in for someone in a teaching situation and how would you handle that situation. The impromptu teaching moved full steam ahead as planned.

Each student impromptu taught. Many students taught with guarded ease. When they were finished the teaching, many expressed a genuine gladness that the experience was over. There was also an expression of that was not so bad, and I think I can do this again. Other students were horrified by the experience and stated that the assignment was unnecessary and had nothing to do with their teaching abilities.

Each student was orally critiqued by their peers and by me. The students were critiqued on what they taught, what was learned from the teaching by their peers, and how they projected their lesson. The feedback was that of support and making suggestions for next time. It was not a pass/fail possibility. Individual grades would not be affected by the experience. The impromptu teaching was a wake-up call addressing unexpected situations in a real classroom-teaching situation.

What is unique about the impromptu teaching is there are times when we are called upon to teach, and we do not have prepared lessons and must teach anyhow. How do new teachers begin to achieve confidence in their own abilities to teach? The confidence usually begins to happen during student teaching/practicum. Practicum students ask questions of their cooperating teacher and supervisor about how they are doing and what they need to change. What works for a particular lesson, and what does not work in terms of approach and lesson implementation.

Before digressing too much, let me return to the present seminar class of nine students. Seven of the nine students had a variety of impressions about the impromptu teaching assignment of the previous semester. Two or three of the students reflected in their evaluations a discomfort with the assignment and, more importantly discomfort with the instructor and my approach to teaching and learning.

For the first class session, I expressed my responses to the evaluations given for the previous class. I stated that teaching is more than planning and teaching lesson plans. Teaching is understanding who you are in the process. It is knowing what your strengths and weaknesses are in teaching and learning. It is having a comfort level about your ethnic heritage. It is knowing about the children you teach from a cultural, ethnic, and diversity perspective.

It is plain and simple. Do some homework to find out who you are teaching. Who are you, and what ethnic heritage do you bring to the classroom? With your cultural background and heritage, what prejudices, biases, and stereotypes do you have and do your students have?

Setting the stage for honest and, in some cases, painful disclosure of ethnicity and stereotypes would be an added ingredient to the seminar class. How to begin the dialogue, and what I want my students to know about themselves and the students they taught. I first visited all of the practicum sites twice. Second, early on in the semester, I asked the student teachers to find out who were the students they taught in terms of diversity and culture. I did not want to know individual histories but general information about their students' ethnic backgrounds. They were asked to find out what was the ethnic background of the students they taught. Many of the nine students had already made assumptions about who their students were.

They shared those assumptions in class. They initially used students' last names and skin color to determine ethnic backgrounds.

Second, each student teacher created a questionnaire for their individual class to fill out and give back to them. What students found out was they were wrong on many accounts about their students' ethnic background. They found out they cannot just go on last name and skin color to determine ethnic background. They found out that they had made erroneous assumptions about ethnic backgrounds, and they did not know much about the erroneous assumptions that they had made.

Case in point: Once, a student teacher believed that all her students of color were African American. Once the questionnaire was distributed and collected, she found that she had several ethnic groups in her class, and African American was not the only group. In fact, African American students were fewer in number than other groups of color represented in the class. When the student shared her findings, she was totally shocked at how incorrect she was to begin with, and second, she had placed all the students into one category—African American.

Several things happened; she began to address her prejudices about the African American students and found that her assessment was unfair and not well based. Second, she realized that the new groupings were from other places in the world. They were from Cape Verde, Haiti, Barbados, and other islands in the Caribbean.

As she did more research about the various people of color in her classroom, her vision of herself and her interactions broadened. Her approach to lessons became more inclusive, and her understanding about her students' ethnicity became one of appreciation and amazement. She also had to look at her own ethnic background and family history. This revealed some learned behaviors about what she had heard and been told while growing up about people of color—especially African Americans. She has commented several times that she just did not know about the different groups of children in her classroom and furthermore had not given it any thought. She is assured now that she cannot afford to make assumptions about students in any classroom. She had to confront her own misinformation and begin to change some thought patterns. She was willing to do the work. Information is needed, and one must continuously check the information and be in contact with their own ethnic realities as they teach and learn.

As the practicum students reveal their research in the practicum course, there is a reality of excitement and relief. Other students in the seminar class are having similar realizations about their Caucasians, Asians, and students of color in the student-teaching classrooms. Distinguishing and knowing the difference between Korean, Chinese, Japanese, and other students from Asian ancestry is important from a point of respect and communication. Not calling all students "Asian" with no concern for country or origin of birthright is culturally irresponsible and insensitive to say the least. Cultural heritage and cultural ethnicity are important factors in creating levels of respect and understanding for the students one teaches. Excitement to learn something new and different about Asian cultures and a relief at mistakes do not have to be made about unfounded assumptions about student ethnic groups.

To refer to all Caucasian students as white and not acknowledge their ethnic history does a disservice to the Caucasian students. The disservice is putting everyone in the same category. It is not honoring diversity and ethnicity. The Caucasian students are from England, France, Germany, Ireland, Canada, and other regions of the world. Learning about each of the ethnic groups and their cultural heritage broadens the practicum students' view of the world. It is no longer using the language of black and white, but rather giving students an identity that transcends the color of one's skin.

Even small children do not define themselves as simply black/white when permitted to have the conversation and cultural experiences in the classroom that go beyond what one looks like. There are resources that can be used to provide experiences in the classroom for building cultural awareness and positive responsiveness about people on a global stage. There are books, short stories, videos, plays, musicals, arts, dances, individual histories, family legacies, guest presenters, Internet searches, community resources, and places of worship that support and enhance student experiences in cultural-diversity teaching and learning.

Teaching Domains

While teaching, it is important to create the environment for students and teachers to be valued. Understanding curricula goals and objectives for effective lessons lead to students' involvement in their learning. Learning environments need to be supportive of the myriad of learning styles in the classroom. How are students involved in learning assignments? Is the work challenging? Is there student ownership for their behavior in classrooms? Is there a sense that the classroom belongs to students as well as teachers?

Dwyer (1991) identifies four domains of instruction at which "good" teachers excel: (1) teaching for content knowledge, (2) teaching for student learning, (3) creating a classroom community conducive to student learning, and (4) displaying a teacher professionalism. Villegas (1991) has extended these four domains for teachers who serve a student population that is culturally and linguistically diverse. She suggests that "good" teachers in these classroom contexts incorporate culturally responsive pedagogy, meaning that they adjust their teaching strategies in response to the learning styles of individual students.

Concern for the effectiveness of teachers is not new. From the earliest days of education program evaluation, the quality of the instructional staff has been considered a significant feature (Heath 1982 and Ladsen-Billings 1994). Unfortunately, for programs serving students of minority status, the evaluation of "effectiveness" has lately been consumed by an empirical concern for multicultural representation in the content of curriculum at the expense of an examination of teaching strategies themselves.

For programs dealing with students with limited English proficiency, interest has centered only on the use or nonuse of students' native language and the development of English-language skills (August and Garcia, 1988). Very little consideration is given to the attributes desired in the professional and paraprofessional staff members who implement the myriad of program types that serve students in compensatory education (Garcia 2001 35).

Redefining the Teacher's Role

Instructors must become familiar with the cognitive, social, and cultural dimensions of learning. We need to recognize the ways in which instructional assessment and evaluation practices affect learning. We should become aware of the purpose and degree of implementation of the classroom curriculum and understand its full impact on students. Teachers must question myths about learning processes and about the potentially under-prepared student. We must debunk myths about students who come from households of lower socioeconomic status or ones where English is not the primary language (Garcia 2001 122). So what do you do as a teacher about the myths? Teachers do research about culture and ethnicity. They form discussion groups in their schools and communities to share information. Teachers invite speakers to their classrooms to share stories, legacies, and events that influence social issues. Teachers begin to tell their stories of their culture to students. Teachers provide a forum in their classrooms for students to share their legacies and cultures and get parents involved as well as senior members of the community in class presentations about culture, ethnicity, and diversity.

As I continue to teach classroom teachers, school administrators, counselors, social/human relations professionals, and managers in the area of cultural diversity and facilitate workshops for various organizations, I believe acknowledging and understanding cultural diversity are an integral part for teaching and learning. The acknowledging and understanding can be supported by reading more, talking more, and questioning more about ethnic groups, their traditions and beliefs. It must be realized that teachers and students are dealing with so many concerns in their learning environments. Many of the concerns of students include retention, peer pressures, peer approval, self-esteem, readiness, racism, sexism, educational tracking, special education, bilingual education, linguistic diversity, cultural differences, attitudes, drugs, divorce, violence, health, death and dying, housing (and the lack of it), jobs, and joblessness.

For teachers, the concerns in many cases are teacher contracts, local, state, and national-budget issues, educational program cuts, diverse populations in the classroom, teacher testing, and student testing. Teachers and students over the last decade have experienced the aftermath of the Persian Gulf War, the end of the Cold War, genocide, and slavery in parts of Africa, Middle East, Philippines, Bosnia/Croatia, and the September 11, 2001, (destruction of World Trade Center in New York/parts of the Pentagon in Washington DC), numerous acts of terrorism, biochemical warfare, and racism revisited on a world stage as well as a local, state, and national stages.

There are a myriad of questions and as many answers to contemplate about the world we live in and how we survive and flourish in the classroom and home. With these concerns, many teachers have come face-to-face with their own realities of who they are and how or why they respond to students and events as they do.

Teachers from all over the country have experienced through teaching, course discussions, and course presentations a practical and humanistic approach to teaching within their curriculum various aspects of multicultural diversity. A practical and humanistic approach includes acknowledging students' learning styles and incorporating teaching methods appropriate to age, linguistic diversity, and cognitive determinations.

A practical and humanistic approach to teaching in the classroom involves teaching students as people who need to be respected, valued, and encouraged to learn. Valuing students' individuality allows students to question and respond to various learning instructions. Teacher attitudes contribute immensely to how students make connections to what is taught and their own perceptions of self.

A prevocational, tech educator has learned that through experiences and education, a lot of prejudices/biases and stereotypes are unfounded. Therefore, education is the key in eliminating these prejudices and biases. You cannot judge a book by its cover. Another suburban educator believes that stereotypes go hand in hand with prejudices. She has learned that no stereotypes are good/positive because people want to be judged as individuals. I don't like it when people make generalizations about me based on my ethnicity (Jewish).

What do I do about other people's generalizations? At first, though, not much. But when I am really pressed to move beyond this point, I really have to want to address other people's beliefs. Once I have decided that I want to address their beliefs, I guardedly ask for more information. I tell them that they are categorizing whole groups of people and not allowing for individual differences in particular groups. I realize that I do the same thing and need to stop that behavior. It is hard to change, and it is hard for others to change also.

Gender Challenges and Academic Performance

Most teachers are beginning to concern themselves with the self-worth of the children as well as the child's achievement. The ability to convey what a student has learned goes a long way toward building self-esteem. After all, shouldn't schools be in the business of training and preparing students to improve their abilities as well as believe that they get what they pay for? (Gwin 1990, 16).

We certainly have not taught enough black boys and girls that self-respect is earned, often with various difficulties. The fact remains that when children have high achievement, they usually feel good about themselves and usually display acceptable behavior. Hand in hand with self-esteem building are the differences in learning styles of boys and girls. While girls perform better in interactive or cooperative groups, boys rise to the challenge of competition. Boys also are more inclined to explore, learn by trial and error, and take risks in volunteering answers (Manuel 1991 22).

It is suggested by Sadker (1991 76:2) for teachers to de-sex-desegregate your classes. Boys and girls usually sit in same-sex clusters. Then during class projects, the teacher tends to gravitate to the boys' clump, and the girls become invisible. There are several techniques teachers can use to address this. Use longer wait—times. Girls tend to be more shy and quiet than boys. Wait three to five seconds, instead of one second, for their answers.

Do not call on boys more often than girls as a classroom-management strategy. Girls tend to be better behaved in class; teachers fall into the trap of calling on the boys to keep them out of trouble. Do not rely on volunteers; they are more likely to be boys. Girls have answers even when they do not have the courage to raise their hands. Gender differences in learning and participating in classrooms are important to acknowledge so educators can be more effective in responding to students who approach discussions and activities in various ways (Sadker 1991).

Teachers can have a prepared list of student names with girl-boy, girl-boy order. The order is used to call on students during a lesson. One can also instruct students when called on to choose someone from a different gender than themselves.

Encourage students to call on each other for the next response in class. At the end of an activity ask, how many boys responded and how many girls responded. See if there is a pattern to student respondents. Ask the class how they want to be called on during certain assignments. Use a couch ball that is handed or thrown to various students before they make contribute to the discussion.

Cultural Diversity in the Classroom

Cultural diversity and racial/ethnic/gender prejudices are parallel ideas. When brought together in learning and teaching arena, much happens for and to the learner and teacher. Cultural diversity as stated in "Cultural Diversity in the Classroom" relates to different cultures that are represented by students, teachers, and administrators in a learning environment. One aspect of cultural diversity is the studying, talking, and sharing about individual backgrounds and legacies in order to develop meaningful and supportive relationships. The sharing and discussing of cultural legacies/ backgrounds allows teachers to listen to their own histories and question others in a group-learning environment. When teachers share their legacies, they come face to face with long-time prejudices and biases, as well as their learned values and individual strengths (Davis Fuller 1992, 7).

Racial/ethnic/gender prejudices are the result of learned behaviors that negatively affect individuals and groups of people. It is the author's belief that people are not born prejudiced, but rather people are taught to be prejudiced. Being prejudiced lends itself to the belief of some stereotypes about others and ourselves.

Teachers need to unlearn certain prejudices and stereotypes. First, there is the acknowledgement of learned beliefs. Of the learned beliefs, which ones really get in the way of treating students fairly and honestly? Which beliefs about certain groups allow for low or no expectations from the learner? Which beliefs allow teachers to not see beyond one's ethnic background or culture? Which beliefs permits teachers to make excuses for students and pass judgments about students that are unfounded for individual students? Teachers need to do some homework. They need to find out how their own stereotypes continue to foster incorrect assumptions about students. To believe that all students from a particular culture, ethnic background behave and/or respond in certain ways limits students' possibilities for success in class.

Second, teachers need to restructure their lessons to be inclusive to various learning styles. Third, teachers need to think about and create questions for inquiry that do not shut down the learner. For instance, "I hope you know the answer," or "What do you think you know about this?" are negative approaches to finding out information. More supportive question would be "Tell me or show me what you know," or "Explain what you know by examples, not definition."

Teachers Need Cross-Cultural Sensitivity

Teachers cannot rely on the cultural knowledge appropriate to their own social groups if they want to work effectively in the multicultural classroom in which children from many ethnic groups may be present. Teachers need to be sensitive to the possible ways that the cultures of students may influence their behaviors, perceptions, and attitudes (Banks and Banks, 42). Teachers must be aware that children from different cultural backgrounds have been "programmed" with their group's subjective culture during their enculturation. Subjective culture is defined by Harry Triandis as the characteristic way in which a cultural group perceives and responds to its social environment. The conscientious teacher will learn about the subjective culture of the children in the class. This knowledge will give the teacher a basis from which to make a value judgment about whether an apparently objectionable cultural custom can be condoned (Banks and Banks 43-44).

Teachers teaching in diverse classrooms are responsible for looking closely and carefully at their own perceptions of groups. What preconceived notions and beliefs are daily demonstrated when interacting with students and professional peers? Are there certain prejudices and biases that teachers have while teaching their various subject matters? Prejudice suggests an active choosing of an ideology, person (group), item, beliefs for or against other choices. Prejudice is a form of discriminating or selecting out that which is not to one's liking or choosing. The process of prejudice behavior is many times bases on stereotyping and preconceived judgment making.

Prejudice alone is not responsible for large-scale social discrimination. It is prejudice and institutional power that, together, create social discrimination—the combination of personal superiority/inferiority belief system and the power to impose that system on others. Without institutional power, we all have about the same ability to inflict pain on others with our prejudices. With the help of institutional power to reinforce biased belief systems and to disadvantage others, we transform prejudice into the destructive "isms": ageism, colorism, ethnocentrism, heterosexism, racism, and/or sexism (Banks and Banks 1993, 4:71).

Stereotypes Effect on Others

A stereotype is a judgment made about a group of people. Stereotypes are negative and make people feel inferior. Stereotypes promote prejudices/ biases and vice versa because oppression is a cycle. The reason why both exist is because individuals and groups make assumptions and judgments. I learned the best way to confront my own prejudices/biases and stereotypes was to be exposed to them. For example, if I felt uncomfortable around old people because I thought they were all mean, I would confront my thoughts, and going to a nursing home for a few visits would help me conclude that my beliefs are not always true.

Stereotypes are used to reinforce fundamental prejudices and our personal superiority/inferiority beliefs about others. These stereotypes are passed down through generations of ethnic groups by word or mouth—through nonverbal communications, by way of personal fears, and misinformation by social practices that exclude one group from another. The effect of stereotypes on individuals and groups of people has a devastating and long-lasting effect on people in general.

Personal experiences also help mold stereotypes. For example, a teacher has two Asian children in their class that excel in mathematics. The teacher brings their taxes to an Asian account and receives the largest tax return thus far in their teaching career. At this point, the teacher truly believes that Asians have strong mathematics abilities. The following school year, the same teacher has an Asian student that needs some extra explanation in mathematics. The student's needs are overlooked. The teacher cannot understand why this Asian student did not pass the mathematics benchmark exam given by the city at the end of the year. Thus, the cycle of stereotyping continues.

An urban public school educator shared this experience and believed stereotypes are a mind conditioned to assumptions based on characteristics regarding a person's ethnicity, physical appearance, religion, age, and sex. The assumptions are derived from influences such as the media, peers, family, or other hierarchy influences.

- What do children see and hear on television?
- What do children hear their parents say whole talking or watching the news?
- Do all peer groups help foster and accept a multicultural world?

This can be changed. Teachers, parents, administrators must work individually and collectively to make the kind of change that is needed. The effort must be joint and ongoing. There must be teacher-development programs that focus on the learner and ethnic-cultural excellence in learning. Teachers must do their homework about ethnic groups in their classrooms. Parents must have cross-cultural literature when possible in their homes that represent images that affirm other ethnic groups and their beliefs. Administrators must make themselves, as well as their faculties, accountable for cross-cultural teaching and planning.

Most teachers know little about different ethnic groups' lifestyles or learning habits and preferences. They tend to be insecure and uncertain about working with African American, Hispanic, Asian, and American Indian students and to have low expectations of achievement for these students. Too many teachers still believe that minority students either are culturally deprived and should be re-mediated by using middle-class whites as the appropriate norm or do not have the capacity to learn as well as Anglos. Teachers form expectations about children based directly upon race and social class—pupil test scores, appearance, language style, speed of task performance, and behavior characteristics, which are themselves culturally defined. Teacher expectations are more influenced by negative information about pupil characteristics than positive data. Teachers transmit these attitudes and expectations in everything they say and do in the classroom (Banks and Banks 1993, 185).

Stereotypes, as discussed in the cultural diversity course taught at the graduate level, have been defined over the years by graduate students as an uninformed but real feeling of superiority/inferiority about people who are not members of the defining group. Stereotypes are prejudices and dislikes of certain people based on how they act, look, live, worship, dress, and speak. Stereotypes are usually negative descriptors of people that many times we do not know.

In other instances, teachers work side by side with professionals from the same or different ethnic/cultural background for which stereotypes exist in their lives. In the workplace, teachers can also create integrated groups in the class to work on various assignments.

1. Using cooperative learning techniques for class assignments permits cross-cultural groups to work together. Cooperative learning groups are concerned with role and responsibility for a task in a group. Have students share roles and responsibilities in the classroom.
2. Rotate groups of children to work with others in the classroom that they may not normally work with for a task. Children may have some ideas of their own. Ask students about their working partners and group presentations.
3. Make assignments of different lengths. Give some long-term assignments and some short-term assignments.
4. Give students a rubric to work with and teach them how to create their own rubrics for particular lessons.

Teachers and student teachers must be responsible for their teaching/learning styles in the classroom. The responsibility to teach all students and be prepared from a curriculum point of view is part of the definition in teaching excellence. Dealing with biases, prejudices, and stereotypes in the classroom calls on teachers to understand their own diversity issues and concerns. Teachers need to do their homework and find out about ethnicity and culture. Teachers need to continuously raise questions about who am I, and who am I teaching? from a cultural perspective. What biases and prejudices do I own, and how can I work with myself to erase those biases and prejudices?

More than Their Best: Personal Learning

For nearly three decades, contemporary and historical issues about multiculturalism have fascinated and challenged me. I have examined, questioned, taught, and finally written about individual and group perceptions on cultural differences and similarities. The fascination has to do with being an African American woman with family, friends, and people who have withstood untold and, in many cases, told stories of pain, suffering, and triumph over the odds.

Living and working in a culture and larger society that has labeled, debased, condemned, lynched, emasculated, and murdered generations of people of color have been disturbing, frustrating, and most of all, unsettling. There is the need to know more history. There is a need to learn these peoples' stories. There is the reality of honoring my ancestors. There is a need to understand cultural/ethnic history so the present will challenge the future to be responsive to cultural/ethnic legacies in an affirmative manner. The stories represent the survival, existence, and sheer will to live and oftentimes thrive.

Being from a family whose mother worked in the home and father worked outside the home for their three children—two younger brothers and myself—to succeed in the world as productive adults is a testament unto itself. The legacy given to each of us was that we were worthy of what we achieved. My parents did more than the very best for us.

My youngest brother is a middle/ high school history teacher in a private school in Philadelphia for more than twenty years and an accomplished musician. He is the family historian, as well. My middle brother is a retired master electrician from the Philadelphia public schools, an independent contractor, an electrical-code instructor and an enterpreneur. I am very proud of my brothers and their accomplishments. They have emotionally and spiritually supported me in my life. We have given to each other the encouragement to "go for it" in our personal and professional lives. There have been disappointments as well as extreme joys. Through it all, we have stood together and genuinely loved and cared about what happened to each other in our lives.

While growing up, there were the chores, the church services on Sunday—every Sunday—church Bible school, church plays/programs, youth activities, and leadership trainings. Each of the activities assisted us in our faith building and self-identity. There were also church ushering, teaching Sunday school, playing piano for Sunday school service, daily school activities, neighborhood activities, and music (clarinet, piano, pipe, organ) lessons. Other activities included having library memberships, reading numerous books, and storytelling by a small group of relatives and close friends. There were also the neighborhood gardens, homemade grape jelly each year, constant baking, home-cooked meals, and Sunday dinner with family. The memory of each of these experiences brings to the forefront a reality of reflective sadness, wholeness, pleasure, and renewed strength.

As I reflect on my years growing up in West Philadelphia, it is clear that the painstaking teachings, reprimands when necessary, intermittent praises, continuous telling and retelling the story of displacement, and escape from slavery in the past and present-day times are daily played out in numerous ways. Likewise, growing up in an African American neighborhood with shopkeepers—who were predominantly Jewish, German, and Polish—I observed that these shopkeepers made their money in our community but spent their profits in their own communities. The homeowners worked hard to pay twice as much for their mortgages as their Caucasian counterparts in other neighborhoods. The black-owned business people represented many who were not able to buy the property where their businesses were located. There are services from the city that had to be continuously asked for by residents. The residents created neighborhood watches and cleaned up their own neighborhoods. The residents created beautiful neighborhood gardens and sitting areas for themselves.

From my family and close neighbors, the story of hard work and just rewards provided on earth and in heaven were a constant reminder to perform well in whatever we did. The carrying on of the family name and not embarrassing or bringing shame on or into the home was stressed daily. Striving to do your best and do better than others before you and, of course, doing better and working harder than others was required and expected.

Being an undergraduate student, teaching in the public schools in Philadelphia, going to graduate school, and continuing to teach students across cultural, ethnic, religious, social-economical/educational levels, and religious beliefs have been a special privilege. The privilege and opportunity to talk, listen, agree, and disagree with hundreds of teachers and professionals on the topic of teaching/learning and managing one's own biases/prejudices has been exhausting and rewarding.

What have I learned from the varied experiences? I have learned that having a strong, religious, caring, and supportive family is more than half the battle in surviving the realities of living and making it. I have learned that worship and community can and do have strengths that surpass daily routines. I have learned that sheer faith and belief in one's self and family allowed me to move past my neighborhood and seek another world that in time would acknowledge my presence. I have learned to value my family, my former neighborhood, friends, and myself. I have learned and continued to experience the importance of different people's belief systems and how they relate to cultural diversity and ethnicity. I have learned how to teach what I know and learn from others of similar and different ethnic backgrounds.

A Quiet Stone

In recent memory, I had an experience while worshiping at my church that caused me reflection and amazement. The more I acknowledged the experience, the more it became evident that this was a statement of who I am to others I have taught. A former graduate student and present teacher in the Boston Public Schools system whispered in my ear, "You are a quiet stone."

Images raced through my mind, and I turned to my friend and former student and responded, "What an amazing thing to say." She spoke back saying, "It's true, you are a quiet stone. You would never have such an elaborate introduction." She was referring to the speaker of the hour and the elaborate introduction given about the keynoter to the worshipers. I have marveled at the comment and thought—a stone—what kind of stone? What shape stone? A quiet stone brings many images to mind. What does the stone represent? Stones and rocks, I have always liked for different reasons.

As a gardener, I am always collecting stones and rocks to rest among the flowers in my garden. The shapes and textures of the stones are sometimes soothing and other times abrasive. The words stayed with me as the service ended, and I continued on with my day.

The statement has bridged my thoughts of strength and continued seeking faith in my beliefs. Being prayerful and learning how to continually listen and grow have become a way of life for me. In teaching teachers and other professionals, it is listening and responding to ways of approaching our own biases and prejudices in ourselves and in others that inspire and motivate me.

Crossing the Street

Not long ago I was standing outside a building just watching people. It was near dusk, and a Caucasian woman was walking her dog. As she walked up the street, she eyed me. She stopped in her tracks, directed the dog to cross the street. I smiled to myself. One, I am not fond of dogs, so the crossing of the street worked well for me. Beyond this, the crossing of the street represented fear for the woman, I suppose. Would she be bothered or more seriously attacked by me? What was going through her mind? For me, what did I have on my person or in my dress or in the color of my skin that provoked her to change her course of walking?

Yes, I smiled, but I also became disgusted. I thought, you do not know me and have made some assumptions about me based on your choice to cross the street. Oh, well, what do I do? Don't ponder or spend too much time on this. Move along, you do have something else to do right now. It does not change the occurrence. It adds to my experiences of living. Did everyone walking on that street cross over to the other side? No, some never looked up, and others just did not see me at all as they walked by.

It is seemingly a small event; but when repeated over a day, a week, a month, a year, it adds up—the fears that individuals and groups walk, run, drive, fly, and move around, which affect others all the time in a myriad of ways. I conscientiously decided many years ago that if I was to be honest and effective in my teaching, I would have to acknowledge my prejudices/biases and find the reasons for them and then decide, what do I want to do about them, and what am I able to do about them? My answer was to read and talk more with others who are willing to discuss race, hatred, prejudices, societal repressions, and related topics in various arenas—the home, school, church, friends' houses, and gathering places.

I decided many years ago to not play the "blame game," the "you owe me" game, the "look what you have done to me and others like me" game, the "I'm not worthy" game, and instead look into my being and not own negative, nonproductive attitudes. I have changed my belief system to affirm who I am. Second, I believe in the teachings of my childhood that included goodness, hard work, patience, integrity, not passing judgments, and faith.

When asked what can others do. The answer is fairly simple. Know what you want to do about your prejudices and find out how you are able to change them. Do more reading and have discussion groups in your workplace, home, place of worship, or community.

It is an ongoing reality coming face-to-face with my own prejudices, biases that continue even now as I teach and interface with my students, colleagues, associates, and friends. The clear notion of working with myself so I can be more effective with others is never finished. There are many successes, and there are letdowns. I am of the affirmative belief that the effort is worth the positive outcomes.

Each course I teach, I learn something about myself and my students. I see, hear, and feel what my students articulate and share about their experiences. This is a hard, tedious work and cannot be managed only in a two-hour, three-day workshop or one-semester course. It is lifelong. It is ever-challenging. It is necessary.

The confronting of my own biases, prejudices, and fears occurs at the waking of the morning hours through the closing of day every day. My faith is my constant companion, and my prayers are for continued resolve and strength to learn/teach. There are the moments of growth and satisfaction in knowing that I am responsible for my feelings, my affect with others and the messages I send myself. This has much to do with my responsibility in acknowledging and going beyond tolerance, useful existence, and continuous reflection for my own awareness and growth.

Teaching about cultural diversity is a lifelong pursuit. It can be accomplished with patience and personal ownership for one's behavior and thinking. It is making choices with students that do not limit what students can do because of their ethnical cultural backgrounds, but rather encouraging students and teachers to achieve because they can.

Each person in the learning environment is encouraged to share information that they want others to know about themselves. This can be done in a variety of ways. The person may use pictures, drawings, music, native costumes, video, cassette tapes, powerpoint presentations, artifacts, and guests or members of the family. The tone set in learning environment or these preparations is quite important.

The teacher and student must be comfortable and feel safe about the ethnic sharing experience as well as the information to be shared. Persons should be encouraged to participate if they choose not share at a specific time. A time limit of fifteen to twenty minutes should be set. Many will not honor that time limit, and that is quite all right. Concrete reasons should be given to the class introducing the ethnic sharing activity. For example, the class has been studying a particular topic in social studies, science, math, language arts, or any subject; and we need to begin as a class to appreciate their own strengths and family legacies, ethnic support for success, and faith in God so that achievements are realized.

CHAPTER SIX

Classroom Management and Cultural Diversity that Enhances Classroom Teaching

Many learners experience understanding the privilege and oppressed parts of their won identity, recovering from and reclaiming parts of that identity in a positive way as a spiritual experience.

—Elizabeth Tisdell

The cultural diversity of students in the classroom is an important aspect of classroom management. Issues related to teacher-student interactions and effective teaching methods in the classroom are important in planning and implementing lessons. What is classroom management as it relates to student learning? Are there rules and regulations in the classroom that the group and individual can identify? Are there expectations for students and teachers that each acknowledges? Is there fairness and consistency in how situations are managed? Is peaceable conflict a goal in the classroom? Is there equity in the classroom with regard to gender, ethnicity, age, content mastery, and learning ability and capability? These questions influence the teaching styles and attitudes of many teachers in the classroom.

Teaching Expectations

There are expectations for teaching and learning about cultural diversity and self-esteem in the classroom. The expectations are what the teacher and students should aim for in the classroom. Expectations strongly suggest that there are clear goals to be reached. Teaching and learning does not occur in a vacuum. There are relationships between content and affect, between ability and capability, and between knowing and learning. The relationships are connected to expectations.

Expectations for Teaching and Learning About Cultural Diversity and Self-Esteem in the Classroom

In addition to the discourse on self-esteem shared earlier in this text, it is important to highlight the expectations for teaching and learning in a culturally diverse learning environment.

1. Sharing information about one's self so that others can and will understand who you are in relationship to themselves and others.
2. Realizing that each member of the class or group has a heritage, legacy, and history that span over hundreds of years.
3. Respecting cultural values and ethnic strengths to support various learning styles.
4. Listening and sharing cultural and gender experiences in the classroom to encourage effective ways of communicating.

5. Understanding our own individual cultural diversity and learning styles in order to achieve in the learning environment.
6. Valuing differences in the learning environment allows each member of the group to appreciate self and others.
7. Acknowledging individual abilities and capabilities so that maximum learning occurs.
8. Realizing one's own identity and purpose (worth) in the learning environment in order to achieve personal and group goals.

Race, Ethnicity, and Stereotypes

Addressing and confronting concepts, beliefs, and actual individual and group behaviors about race and ethnicity are vitally important in learning environments. Acknowledging one's biases and prejudices and working to rid one's self from biases and prejudices can provide a freeing-up and moving-forward attitude to dealing with students, parents, and other educators from a position of encouragement and social justice.

There are stereotypes that are attributed to most ethnic groups. It is a contention that stereotypes serve several purposes in our lives. One, they permit biases and prejudices to influence our attitudes and treatment of people who are like us and not like us. Stereotypes give reason to not engage in meaningful dialogues and/or to have healthy interactions one with the other. It builds and maintains territorial walls for limited engagements—if there are engagements at all. Biases and prejudices are not exclusive to one group. They are fostered and reinforced from birth. In many cases, they are created to protect and keep one safe. Biases and prejudices are perpetuated through family relationships, religious groups, interrelational and intrarelational groups, communal affiliations that support definitive ideologies, norms, beliefs, and best practices.

Case in point: If you have a negative feeling and attitude about certain foods and you believe that eating that food will harm you in some way, and you practice that eating that food is not good for you, then you have created a prejudice toward that particular food. You may never have really tasted that food; but because of your feelings, you just know it is harmful. The same scenario can be used with people that we have not had a relationship with or not spent time with in our lives. The biases and prejudices lead to unfounded stereotypes that are attributed to more than one person in a particular group but to an entire group. In the classroom/learning environment, experiencing biases and prejudices are a daily occurrence. Some are subtle in nature while others are quite overt.

Spoken language, dialect, nonverbal communication, and body language are ways that various attitudes, likes, and dislikes are shared in the classroom. In the realm of ethnicity and race, teachers, students, parents, professional assistants, education specialists, principals/headmasters, department chairs, superintendents, school committees, and community liaisons and workers need to understand the dynamics of people and group/individual responses to situations that influence learning and teaching. There is a need to understand heritage and legacy related to students of color and other ethnic groups in the classroom. The questions of class and caste are essential earmarks of group acceptance and group/individual upward mobility on a social, economic, political, and educational scale.

Educators need to have discussions, read diversified material, and do their own research concerning race and ethnic groups. It is important for educators and related professionals to be more enlightened and have understanding for the children they teach.

What is often overlooked in the education setting when discussing issues such as racism or sexism is a positioning of individuals within the discussion. Confronting one's own position, as a student or an educator, within whiteness could mean being implicated as a member of the group that perpetuates and benefits from a system of oppression. Yet it could also mean recognizing the life-determining negative effects whiteness has on one's own group. (Multicultural Perspective, 8:53)

You are the conduit, the vessel, the steward, the connection, the relay, and the tool by which teaching occurs. You are not the subject but the verb—even though most of the words describing you, naming you are nouns. You are the verb—the direct actor or indirect receiver of the verb.

Just teach, know, understand, listen, speak, be still, be emotional, contribute, research, plan, implement, question, answer, sigh, frown, laugh, cry, pout, move away, move forward, pause, hiccup, growl, scream, pray, shake your head, stare, roll your eyes, smirk, gasp, and so on—whatever it takes within reason to participate in the learning and knowing process.

Teaching is clearly about the children, the toddlers, the elementary students, the adolescents, the adult learner, the elder learner—all who gather in a place to receive and share knowledge.

Parenting is discovering and revisiting behaviors and expectations we want for our children. It is creating a value and moral system so that our children will become independent and responsible for their actions. It is developing a sense of pride and goodness that can be accepted and extended to others. It is building trust and "yes, you can" attitudes for achievement and success. It is supporting talent skills and creativity for positive results in our children's lives. It is not knowing all the answers and being steadfast in our convictions of who we are and becoming in our own right. It is for lifelong, with moments of excitement joy, sadness, exhilaration, tears, doubt, fear, laughter, and aloneness. It is finding and keeping faith to weather the elements and travel the road unchartered. It is unconditional love and compassion. It is awesome; at times, it just is.

It is about the children, indeed and with that, we move forward!

The Meaning of Cultural Diversity

Cultural diversity has different meanings and interpretations depending on the field of interest—in education, management, social services, the sciences, modern technologies, government, religious organizations, and neighborhood communities by individuals or groups. Cultural diversity in an educational setting relates to the different cultures that are represented by students, teachers, and administrators in a learning environment. Cultural diversity is the studying and talking about individual backgrounds and legacies in order to develop meaningful and supportive relationships. Having children and teachers share and talk about their ethnic backgrounds and family legacies can be a rich and rewarding experience if teachers are prepared to share their legacies with the classes they teach. Cultural diversity is the interrelationship among values, music, food, ideology, belief, history, legacy, custom, language, dance, and tradition between people.

For most of us, multicultural education has come to mean putting together a special unit or celebration that depicts the cultural heritage of our students. These are often taught in conjunction with special holidays. It is believed that multicultural education should be an everyday thing—something that is woven into every lesson taught. It helps to bridge a gap between home and school. It uses of what is familiar. It motivates and inspires. And it also lets students to have input into what is taught in the classroom, makes learning more interactive, and, therefore, gives more meaning (Zanger 1990 vol. 5).

There are expectations for teaching and learning about cultural diversity and self-esteem in the classroom. The expectations are what the teacher and students should aim for in the classroom. Expectations strongly suggest that there are clear goals to be reached. Teaching and learning do not occur in a vacuum. There are relationships between content and affect, between ability and capability, and between knowing and learning. The relationships are connected to expectations.

> One of the greatest feelings in life is the conviction that you have lived the life you wanted to live—with the rough and the smooth, the good and the bad—but yours, shaped by your own choices and not someone else's. (Michael Ignatieff)

My family possesses a legacy and history of achieving and trusting in each other and demonstrating love, faith, and belief that in life, most things are possible when we have honesty, hard work, and trust in God. Trusting those instincts while deferring judgment in making decisions was an important attribute I learned to understand. Being part of a family that worked hard and smart to instill love, trust, support, know-how, humor, prayer, faith, hope, and assurance of trying is the legacy I extended to my daughter. There are countless episodes, stories, and events that reflect the trust, work ethic, faith, caring, growth, and love in our family.

One such story involves moving to New England, Boston—in particular—from Philadelphia in the early 1970s. It was truly a faith-walk and life-changing decision on my part. My father had ten years earlier suffered a stroke, and my mother was taking care of him and herself. In 1978, he took a turn for the worse. I had just bought my home and was working three jobs to maintain myself. I remember visiting my dad in the intensive care unit at Hospital of the University of Pennsylvania on Thirty-fourth and Spruce Streets. As I sat by his bed with him in his weakened state, I whispered to my dad, "I need you to live just one more year, Dad, so that I can move into my new home." It is important to note that two years before I graduated from undergraduate school, my dad had his stroke in the Sunday-school room at our church in my lap. That was a turning point in my life. So my request was one of love and fear at the same time. The outcome was that one year to the day, my dad stayed alive and died in the fall of 1979. It was a prayer granted. It was trust and love between us. It was a walk of faith. It was family being there for another's accomplishment. It was faith, unconditional love—dad to daughter and vice versa—and belief in God. It was family being just that "family."

Another experience to share: I was in eighth grade; my counselor advised me that I should pursue a business-major course of study in high school. It was commented by the counselor that I did not have the skills needed to pursue a college academic-track curriculum. I remember crying and really wanting to really be in the college academic-track curriculum, and my mother agreed with me. She told the counselor that her daughter should be allowed to enroll in the college-curriculum program. I remember my mom saying, "You should at least be given a chance to try, and if you are not successful, it will not be because you did not try or were denied access. Do not let others decide what your success might be without being given a chance. It is your call, and you should have the opportunity to create your own success." I was able—with the support and love of my mom—to take the college academic-track curriculum. The rest is history. Both these encounters along with countless others have had a lasting impression with me in my life. It keeps me with the attitude and belief "yes, I can" with my family's love, support, and faith in God's unchanging hand.

CHAPTER SEVEN

Cultural Diversity— Cultural Diversity, History and Ethnic America

To have one's individuality completely ignored is like being pushed quite out of life. Like being blown out as one blows out a light.

—Evelyn Scott

Providing the historical point of view is important in beginning the dialogue about cultural diversity from an ethnicity point of view. Having students and teachers discuss ethnicity, race, and gender issues in American history can prove beneficial for the learning and sharing process in cultural diversity. Along with the historical perspective is a discussion concerning education in America (an overview) from 1950 to 1990.

The history of ethnic groups and their passage to the United States reveals in many cases a painful, strife-ridden, demoralizing, struggling, as well as joyful, hopeful, and determined journey. The newcomers to America wanted to achieve a place for themselves as well as establish cultural/family identity and purpose that supported their ideologies and beliefs.

Cultural diversity in the classroom should allow for each person to value differences and similarities of peers and teachers. Each person is entitled to their perceptions and to their opinions. Cultural diversity from a sharing perspective allows each person to be responsive to their own feelings and their own ethnic values. The whole idea is not to point the finger at someone else for their biases and prejudices but, instead, to deal directly with one's own biases and prejudices on one's own terms. The sharing allows individuals to talk about themselves and their families and their activities in given situations. The audiences listening to the sharing play a vital role. The listening perspective allows for questions and quiet reflective thought. There may be laughter as well as tears. There maybe anger, and there may be rage. There must be a supportive atmosphere for the listeners and the sharers. Peers will many times come to the support and aid of the person sharing in unique and supportive ways. The leader's role is that of facilitating the activity, sharing their legacies, and keeping time. At the end of the experience, there can be observations made, questions asked, points cleared up or redefined/explained, and constructive feedback given.

It is also important for the learning group to define cultural diversity from their (the teacher/learner's) experience and perspective in the learning environment so that the individuals in the class have a shared meaning for cultural diversity.

Every decision we make is tested by our values.
—John Sims, Vice President,
Personnel Digital Equipment Corporation

Ethnic America: An Overview

Attitudes, biases, and prejudices have an origin in the larger culture of the United States. It is of major importance not to place, blame, or denounce individuals or ethnic groups for past behaviors, but to have a point of reference in understanding how attitudes and behaviors have come to be. Diane Ravitch writes that where educational oppression of a minority was blatant and purposeful, as in the case of the American Indian, the policy was a disaster that neither educated nor assimilated. Through most of American history, missionaries, and government, officials took it as their duty to civilize and Christianize the Indians; usually, this meant that Indian culture and language and folkways had to be eliminated. While some were "weaned away from the blanket," as the saying goes, most simply developed a strong internal resistance to the new behavior. Forced efforts at assimilation tended to produce precisely the opposite of what was intended.

Christian missionaries tried to bring white civilization to the Indians throughout the colonial period. From 1778 until 1871, the federal government signed treaties with Indian tribes in which the Indians ceded land, and the government pledged various public services such as education and medical care. There were missionary schools that favored bilingual instruction using Indian languages, but after the Civil War, the federal government began to insist on faster assimilation. During the New Deal era—under the leadership of John Collier, commissioner of Indian Affairs from 1933 until 1945—Congress passed an act in 1934 to strengthen tribal self-government, and Collier launched a program of cultural freedom for the Indians.

The story of Indian education in the United States illustrates the variability of the historical experience—even when it is that of a clearly oppressed group. It is a history that most nearly fits the radical concept of education as a tool of coercion and imposition. The very substantial shift to pluralistic policies in the late 1920s and then again in the 1960s underlines the struggle between opposing philosophies and the differences of time periods (Ravitch 1985, 192-197).

Silberman in *Crisis in Black and White* (1964) contends it was only eight years after the founding of the republic when a member of the House of Representatives took the floor to complain about the Riffraff flooding the big cities. "Unrestricted immigration might have been satisfactory when the country was new and unsettled," he declared; but now, the United States had reached maturity and was fully populated—the nation's well-being required an end to immigration. The flood of foreign riffraff had been growing throughout the eighteenth century; it was to remain a recurrent theme down to our own day. As early as 1718, "proper" Bostonians worried that "these confounded Irishmen will eat us all up." And in 1729, a mob prevented the docking of several ships bringing immigrants from Belfast and Londonderry. Pennsylvanians were equally outraged by the flood of German immigrants into their territory; in the middle of the century, the great Benjamin Franklin delivered a number of attacks on the "Palatine Boors"—the Germans, migrating to Pennsylvania. Jefferson, too, opposed mass immigration, fearing that it would expose the new nation to the corrupting influence of a decadent Europe. And the first Congress heard a plea to bar admission of lithe common class of vagrants, paupers, and other outcasts of Europe.

Thirty years later, things seemed to be going from bad to worse. In the next decade, 152,000 immigrants entered the United States—half again as many as in the three preceding decades. Between 1850 and 1860, over 2.5 million immigrants entered the United States. All told, some forty-two million immigrants have settled in the United States since 1820, the first year in which accurate records were kept.

The immigrants came for many reasons. Some to seek political asylum, some because they had been forced off the land by famine or technological change, some because of religious persecution, some because the trip to America was a means of escaping jail or the debtors' prison. In the early years of the nation, some immigrants came because they were literally snatched off the streets of London and other towns to find themselves "slaves"—indentured servants in the new land. But in every period, the immigrants came because the new nation, and especially its growing cities, needed their labor to build its streets and offices, lay its railroad tracks, service its homes and restaurants, and do all the menial jobs that the older residents disdained. For the American city during the past hundred fifty years, the raw material was the stream of immigrants pouring in from Britain, Ireland, Germany, Norway, Italy, Russia, Poland, and a dozen other lands. Thus, most of the huge middle class that dominates American life today was manufactured in the big-city slums of yesteryear. Indeed, a great epoch of American history is now drawing to a close: the epoch of the ethnic groups. Increasingly, the sons and grandsons and great-grandsons of immigrants find their identity through membership in one of the three main religions, as well as through ethnic affiliation (Silberman 1964, 19).

A new epoch was beginning, dominated instead by race. The new immigrants were distinguished from the older residents neither by religion nor by national origin; they were Protestants, for the most part, and could boast of an American ancestry much older than that of the established city dweller. Their sole distinguishing feature was color; the newcomers were black. The Negro migration to the city actually began about one hundred years ago when the Jim Crow system first began to take shape in the South, and white men moved actively and brutally to force the Negro back into his pre-reconstruction place.

Beginning around 1890, the forces that had kept Southern racism and fanaticism in check rapidly weakened and became discredited. In the North, the desire for sectional reconciliation persuaded liberals to drop their interest in the Negro, who was the symbol of sectional strife; increasingly, liberals and former abolitionists began espousing the shibboleths of the Negro's innate inferiority in the pages of the *Atlantic Monthly*, *Harper's*, the *Nation*, and the *North American Review*, and this in turn encouraged the more virulent Southern racists. "Just as the Negro gained his emancipation and new rights through a falling out between white men," wrote historian C. Vann Woodward, "he now stood to lose his rights through the reconciliation of white men." Not only did the Negro serve as a scapegoat to aid the reconciliation of Northern and Southern white men, but he also served the same purpose in aiding the reconciliation of estranged white classes in the South. The battles between the Southern conservatives and radicals had opened wounds that could be healed only by the nostrum of white supremacy (Silberman 1964, 22-23).

Conclusively, in W. E. B. DuBois—a profile edited by Rayford W. Logan—Dr. Booker T. Washington, the founder of Tuskegee Institute, writes that we must recognize American caste prejudice as a fact that cannot be striven against; but to which we must adjust and adapt ourselves just as we recognize the fact of gravitation as one of the immutable facts and laws of nature. To disregard it and jump from a tower or leap over a precipice is to court and meet certain death. So the colored man who clamors for his civil and political rights—who does not lie down, keep still, and remain quiet when the white man of the South tells him to—is as wise as the man who butts his head against a stone wall or as the bull who charges into a locomotive that is coming toward it at full speed, with steam up and throttle valves thrown back.

Dr. W. E. B. DuBois agreed with Dr. Washington in that Dr. DuBois recognized caste prejudice as a basic and fundamental fact of the black man's existence, which cannot be ignored or passed by—by our closing our eyes to it—just as the ostrich does not elude its pursuers by burying its head in the sand and thinking that because it does not see its pursuers, its pursuers cannot see it (Logan 1971, 102).

It was further stated by Professor W. E. B. DuBois that a man is not the slave of circumstances but transforms his environment after the pattern of his ideals. He recognizes that a man by his own attitude may transform the world's estimate of him (Logan 1971, 105).

When the human drama opened, Africans were on the scene and acting. For a long time, in fact, the only people on the scene were Africans. For six hundred thousand years, Africa and Africans led the world. Were these people who gave the world fire and tools and cultivated grain? Were they Negroes? The ancient bones are silent. It is possible, indeed, probably that they were dark-skinned. More than that cannot be said at this time.

Civilization started in the great river valleys of Africa and Asia, in the Fertile Crescent in the Near East and along the narrow ribbon of the Nile in Africa. In the Nile Valley, the beginning was an African as well as an Asian achievement. Negroes, or people who would be considered Negroes today, were among the firsts to use tools, paint pictures, plant seeds, and worship gods. Black people were known and honored throughout the ancient world (Bennett 1962, 5).

The man who emerged from this African chrysalis was a courageous warlike individual. He was not soft, but he was hard. He had fought the tsetse fly, the mosquito, and hundreds of nameless insects—and he had survived. He had wrested from the hungry jungle gaps of land, and he had found time to think beautiful thoughts and to make beautiful things. He was used to hard work, and he was accustomed to an elaborate social code. If he were a nobleman or a rich merchant or a priest—if, in short—he belonged to the upper classes; as did many who came to America in chains, he was used to political responsibility, to giving orders and taking them, to making and altering rules, to governing. In time, as Stanley M. Elkins has said, "He was the product of cultural traditions essentially heroic in nature (Bennett 1962, 17).

John Hope Franklin, the eminent modern-day scholar states, "The survival of varying degrees of African culture in America does not suggest that there has been only a limited adjustment of the Negro to the New World situation; to the contrary, it merely points up the fact that he came out of an experience that was sufficiently entrenched to make possible the persistence 'of some customs and traditions.' After all, perhaps the survival of Africanisms in the New World was as great as it was because of the refusal of the members of the dominant group in America to extend, without reservations, their own culture to the Negroes whom they brought over" (Bennett 1962, 18).

The immigration of Asians to America was pejorative and complex. In 1763, Filipinos were placed into the Manila galleon trade (1565-1815) between Mexico and the Philippines. They settled in Louisiana after jumping ship. They built their villages on stilts and fished for their livelihood. One of the forty-six founders of El Pueblo de Nuestra Señora la Reina de los Angeles del Río de Porciúncula, now the City of Los Angeles in California, was Antonio Miranda Rodriguez of Philippine ancestry. From 1849-1852, the Chinese arrived—some as indentured servants—during the California gold rush. The bulk of Chinese immigrants later became a source of cheap labor to work the railroads, mines, fisheries, farms, orchards, canneries, garment industries, manufacturing of cigars, boots, and other products. There was an exclusion of Chinese from public schools in San Francisco in the mid-eighteen hundreds; and by 1870, the Naturalization Act excluded Chinese from citizenship and prohibited the entry of wives of laborers.

By 1883, the Japanese replaced the Chinese as a source of cheap labor after the Exclusion Act was enforced. By 1910, Angel Island was set up as a detention center for those Asian non-laboring classes desiring entry into the United States. There were long waiting periods under inhumane conditions—suicides on Angel Island occurred. There were discriminatory immigration laws, nationality acts, concentration camps (1942-1944), and the California Alien Land Acts (*A Brief History of Asians in America*, 12-14). From the mid-seventeen hundreds to the present, discrimination against Asian Americans has existed. Asian Americans have struggled and endured.

> The great discovery of my generation is that human beings can alter their lives by altering their attitudes of mind. (Psychologist William James)

Cultural Diversity and the Race Card

Whiteness should not be defined as racism, sexism, classism, or any other ism but rather as an ideology accompanied by action, which both favors white people, predominantly elite and upper class, heterosexual, white males over others and hierarchizes the maintaining whites and people of color by other isms such as gender, class, or sexual orientation. For example, whiteness gives more status to white women as a group than people of color as a group. As a group, poor whites have advantages not available to working-class blacks. One might consider the notion of whiteness as a narcissistic love of being white and structural whiteness as a system of oppression controlled by a power elite comprised of heterosexual white males (Feagin 2000 and Kivel 2004) who normalize "white as right."

Because whiteness is a system of oppression, it is important to find ways to understand its structural nature. Systemic or institutional oppression involves the flowing elements: First, there must be a dominant group, one that dictates and controls the mechanisms of the society. This group both rewards and excludes those under its control with the purpose of self-preservation (Kibei 2004). The dominant group, to be effective and survive, must align itself with those who approximate the imagined and constructed norm to remain both numerically and politically strong. The second group, the support group, has characteristics similar to the dominate group but must have a motivation to remain adhered to the established norm. Members of this group are given relative power, privilege, and advantage that allow them to become bested in the maintenance of the dominant ideology, believing themselves to be members of the dominant group (Wallerstein 1979).

The final element includes those groups whose characteristics, including politics, permanently exclude them as a group from any membership in the previous groups. Those in this group have little, if any, access to the benefits provided by society. Instead, the dominant elites seek to make them pawns playing them against one another while they are working to develop a collective resistance that will challenge the power of the dominant group (Guinier and Torrs 2002, 52).

Oppression at this excluded level rearranges groups based on differences such as race, class, gender, or economic status but not in a linear fashion. Collins (2000) calls this intersectionality of oppression. For example, black people are rarely found in the dominant, support, or borderline groups; yet if a black man is a professional athlete or holds a professional degree, his shirt in economic status may allow him to move more freely and with more privilege in society than other black men.

White feminist women may align with black feminist women, yet the former group holds more privilege than the latter group based solely on phenotypic differences that place the former closer to the established norm.

Poor whites may be excluded to some extent based on class and economic differences, yet usually hold more power than middle-class black families because of phenotypic differences (Multicultural Perspectives 2006, 8:52).

Racial minority groups experienced tension between achieving steady gains in education as reflected in years of schooling obtained, SAT scores and other standardized test scores, and simultaneous lack of economic progress and even erosion of gains in lifestyle, economic status, and rights. For example, between 1970 and 1989, the white and African American education gap closed from 3 years to 2.3 years. At the same time, however, poverty and unemployment in minority communities are harder than white communities. President Bush vetoed the Civil Rights Act of 1990 and the legality of scholarships for minority students was seriously questioned. These occurrences led to growing frustration (*Race Class and Disability in the Classroom*, chap. 3:49).

Most educators do not teach ethnic minority students how to survive and succeed in school—for example, how to study across ethnic learning styles, how to adjust talking styles to accommodate school expectations, how to interact appropriately with school administrators and impact literacy development and educational achievement, which is responsible for insidious social and political marginalization, resulting in blighted lives and unfulfilled opportunities for legions of people (Purcell-Gates, 140).

There is a misconception that Asian Pacific Islanders are socially, financially, and academically successful. This stereotype, known as the model minority, has let to unfair treatment and stifled the needs of many Asian Pacific Islanders subgroups. Peterson, a population expert, once wrote that Japanese Americans were the model minority (Weinberg 1997). Consequently, media took his written information and generalized it for all Asian Pacific Islanders. Asian Pacific Islanders' problems have been glossed over because of the negative effects of the stereotype of the model minority. Media perpetuates the model minority stereotype by misrepresenting the Asian Pacific Islanders as problem-free individual who do not complain or cause trouble (Multicultural Perspectives 2006). The model minority stereotype is contested because Asian Pacific Islanders are susceptible to social problems comparable to those of other ethnic groups. The stereotype creates resentment among other ethnicities who mistakenly believe that Asian Pacific Islander subgroups are more successful. Weinberg (1997) states that conservative white political figures, publishers, and journalists benefited from the promotion of the model minority. It should be noted that under the federal affirmative action regulations, Asian Pacific Islanders were not initially included as a protected minority group (Suzuki 2002).

The academic problems of Asian Pacific Islanders have been neglected and ignored due to the negative effects of the model minority stereotype. Asian Pacific Islanders experience academic problems that are similar to those of other students, which also contradict the notion of the model minority.

There are significant group differences between group and individual learning styles among Asian Pacific Islanders students. Park (1997) reports that small group instruction is supported by Vietnamese and Filipino students. In addition, Chinese, Filipino, and Korean subgroups found visual stimulus to be more helpful to their learning process.

Teachers often do not acknowledge the academic problems of Asian Pacific Islander students because of their acceptance of the model minority stereotype. Asian Pacific Islander subgroups have different cultural values and characteristics that can often be overlooked. Cultural conflicts arise with students' cultural backgrounds are not validated within academic, which can lead to learning difficulties (Poon-McBrayer and Garcia 2000; Multicultural Perspectives 2006, 48).

There is one important caveat to this analysis the least-educated Latino immigrants are those who are unauthorized to work in or reside in the United States. In the 1990s, unauthorized migrants comprised over one-half of the net growth of the total population of the Mexican or Central American foreign-born population. It is estimated that at least two-thirds of all unauthorized migrants did not complete high school, so they make up the preponderance of the total Latino foreign-born population with no more than a primary education. Thus, it is reasonable to conclude that unauthorized Latino migrants contributed disproportionately to the net increase of Latino immigrants in the 1990s with a primary education or less. This means, of course, that the figures in this report understate recent improvements in the education of legally admitted Latinos.

Latino immigrants are often singled out for their low levels of education and an apparent widening educational gap with natives. In fact, they have been closing the gap in high school education and in the future several factors should favor ongoing improvements. There should be increasing secondary completion rates in Latin countries, and the trend should be toward a higher educational profile for immigrants than for the ascending country population overall. In addition, there will be an aging out of older less-educated immigrants. If the immediate past is any indication, in another thirty years or so, Latino immigrants will have an educational profile similar to that of the native-born population today. During that time, natives will no longer be pulling away as quickly as they have in recent decades. Therefore, the educational gap between natives and Latino immigrants ought to close steadily as a result of the confluence of these two trends: Slowing improvement in the native population means it is not likely to continue pulling away, and the educational distribution among immigrants ought to catch up.

Future gains among Latino immigrants will require ongoing increases in secondary education and significant steps forward in college education. Latino immigrants are noted for not "dropping in" to high school; in other words, many who arrive as young adults do not even enroll in American schools. Among those who do enroll, the Latino immigrant high school dropout rate is much higher than that of natives. As more high school-educated immigrants arrive, however, this problem may ease. As education improves individuals' aspirations both here and abroad, for more education should increase. The policy challenge, as always, is to encourage young immigrants to pursue and complete their education. For immigrants who arrive as adults, practical skills trainings, and language instructions remain important tools for success.

In the past, the gap in education between natives and immigrants was blamed on a generous immigration policy that favors family reunification over education. Poorly educated immigrants, who are permitted to petition for family members, tend to attract new immigrants who also have poor education. By contrast, immigrants admitted under the employment preferences of the American immigration system tend to be rather well educated. This dichotomy is unlikely to change, but the findings reported here suggest that even family-based immigration is likely to see improved education among new immigrants.

As far as legal immigration is concerned, the picture should be one of improving trends. But that is not necessarily the case for the substantial inflow of unauthorized migrants well-known to have significantly less education than their legal compatriots. The forces driving educational improvements appear to be less applicable to unauthorized migrants. Historically, they have been drawn from the least-educated populations in Latin America, and they have the least education of any immigrant group in the United

States. So while policymakers need not be as concerned as before about the educational fallout of family reunification, changes in legal immigration policies will not affect the negative impact of unauthorized migration.

Education remains a key to the success of both Latino immigrants in the United States and the communities that receive them. The medium-to-long-term trends in this regard seem positive. For the immediate and foreseeable future, policymakers should not abandon their attempts to assist newcomers through immigrant-friendly schools and adult skills training. Moreover, they should have some confidence that their efforts will not be overwhelmed by a limitless supply of poorly educated Latino immigrants. As the educational profile of the Latino immigrant population continues to improve, education programs aimed at this population should be expected to yield greater results.

Over the past twenty years, some scholars and other observers have decried the low educational profile of Latino immigrants, asserting that the education gap between these newcomers and the native born causes a variety of economic, fiscal, and social ills. Indeed, proponents of reduced immigration from Latin America often cite particularly harsh versions of this line of reasoning. The education gap does exist, and it is a fact that immigrants with little education usually wind up at the bottom of the U.S. labor market.

However, Latino immigrants have, in fact, made notable strides in narrowing the educational gap, and their education profile is likely to continue to improve in the future. The share of high school-educated Latino immigrants has doubled, while the share of those with less than high school has decreased by one-half. Latino immigrants supply a significant and growing share of workers in the United States, and the number of new arrivals is not projected to decline soon. Educational achievement is—and will continue to be—a critical factor in determining whether or not millions of foreign-born Latinos will move forward.

Poorly educated immigrants face daunting job prospects in an epoch when college-educated workers continue to earn higher wages while the earnings of workers with less than high school education fall behind. The resultant increase in inequality associated with educational attainment over the past three decades places immigrants at a double disadvantage. The least skilled workers earn little in today's economy, and they and their families are more often found living in poverty than other Americans. Further, the available research is not clear as to whether Latino immigrants ever earn as much as natives with the same level of education even after the newcomers gain experience in the U.S. labor market. Even if Latino immigrants are able to catch up with equally educated natives, the poor education of many provides them few opportunities to earn a good living.

An abundant supply of low-skilled and low-paid Latino immigrant workers is beneficial to the U.S. economy in several ways, but it can have adverse effects as well. Immigrants comprise a large percentage of all workers with less than high school education, and economic research shows that they compete with native workers who have not completed high school. The growth of this labor force can drive down the wages of low-skilled workers. Indeed, a growing supply of low-skilled immigrant workers can have its most immediate impact on this very same immigrant workforce by depressing wages. While this is not good for those at the low end of the labor market, the availability of these workers helps reduce the costs of producing a wide range of goods and services and thus benefits business owners, investors, and consumers. Additional social impacts develop from a persistent or increasing divide between low—and high-income workers. In an information-based economy, differences in education are powerfully associated with differences in earnings potential.

For several decades, the elderly have made up the least-educated segment of the population among the native born of all racial and ethnic groups. Overall, levels of educational attainment among older Americans offer a reverse image of the enormous gains in education that marked U.S. history in the twentieth century. Older individuals are more likely to have completed their education before desegregation, before Sputnik, before the GI Bill, or before the expansion of the land-grant university system. During the past three decades, a significant percentage of this population aged out of the labor force, and its size declined due to mortality. This demographic process, which is a simple function of the passage of time, steadily improved the educational profile among the native born by reducing the least-educated segment of that population. That process is now substantially complete for the American native-born population.

In the future, that same process will be at work in the Latino immigrant population. Again, the elderly are the least-educated segment of the Latino population, but many of this poorly educated cohort is still of working age. Hence, the attrition of this population will produce notable gains in the educational profile.

One of the key factors in improving the educational profile of the native-born Americans in the last quarter of the twentieth century was the increasing number of women pursuing secondary and postsecondary education. That same change is now being seen among Latino immigrants.

There is a growing population of foreign-born Latinos who come to the United States in their youth and complete their education here. On average, they complete more years of education than immigrants who are schooled abroad. Educational achievement is slowly and steadily improving in Mexico and the rest of Latin America; consequently, the population from which immigrants are drawn has a higher educational profile. Latino immigrants are significantly more educated than Latin Americans who remain in their home countries.

This report describes changes—based on U.S. Census survey data—in the educational profile of Latino immigrants in the United States from 1970 to 2000. All of the discussion herein refers to persons of age twenty-five or more. Children, teenagers, and young adults are often currently enrolled in school; thus, their educational profile is in flux, and they are not part of the analysis. Beyond the young adult years, most people have completed their schooling.

Improved Education of Latino Immigrants

The current population of foreign-born adults has grown to 9.5 million. During the thirty-year period between 1970 and 2000, the percent of Latinos with primary education are less decreased while the share that was more educated increased. By 2000, the biggest share of Latino immigrants had completed secondary education. For example, the share of those with secondary education increased from 18 to 41 percent between 1970 and 2000, while the share of college graduates almost doubled—increasing from 9 to 18.12 percent. The share of adults with primary education or less was predominant in 1970; however, by 2000, the share with secondary education or better had become predominant. These changes produced an improved educational profile of the entire adult Latino immigrant population.

Immigrants Educated in America Are Better Educated

Latino immigrants who are educated in the United States are significantly better educated than those who are educated abroad. Schooling is more universal in America, and foreign-born Latinos who arrive as children usually complete more years of education than immigrants who arrive as adults. However, most Latino immigrants are in their young-adult years when they first settle in the United States and have already completed their education abroad.

In recent years, a greater share of foreign-born Latinos have been immigrating in childhood and completing their education in the United States. Essentially, all Latino immigrants who arrive before age eleven complete an American primary education and most go on to complete high school.

More than 80 percent of American-educated immigrants complete high school or college; that figure is approximately 10 percent points less than the average of the entire United States populace. Nearly 25 percent of American-educated immigrants complete an associate's college degree or better. Very few American-educated immigrants stop with less than primary education. In contrast, only 50 percent of immigrants who are educated abroad completed high school or college, and 33 percent completed no more than primary education. Meanwhile, 18 percent failed to complete primary school.

More of the foreign-born Latino population is educated in America today than three decades ago. The foreign-born Latino population in 1970 included relatively fewer families than in 2000. Over time, the immigrant stream has matured, and more Latino couples settle young enough to raise their families here. Along with family building, enrollment in American schools has increased.

In 1970, only 11 percent of all Latino immigrant adults completed their education in the United States; however, by 2000, that share had doubled. Today, 21 percent of the Latino immigrant adult population is American educated, and they are raising the educational profile of the entire Latino immigrant population. However, immigrants educated abroad are far more numerous than the American educated. Approximately, eight-tenths of today's Latino immigrants have been educated abroad. Immigrants educated abroad comprise 86 percent of the total adult Latino foreign-born population with primary education or less. They are just 40 percent of the total adult Latino foreign-born population that has completed high school or college (Lowell and Sons 2002).

Valuing Differences—A Model

The cultural diversity lessons are based on a valuing-differences model created by Barbara Walker of Digital Equipment Corporation. This model was developed for industry, but works quite well in an educational setting and in classroom management. The valuing differences model includes:

1. Stripping away stereotypes
2. Learning to listen and probe or the differences in people's assumptions
3. Building authentic and significant relationships with people one regards as different
4. Enhancing personal empowerment
5. Exploring and identifying group differences

For each category, a discussion is encouraged about stereotypes—listening to people who are different and understanding how and why people are different or similar from ourselves. Encouraging relationships and the responsibility for relationships outside our own groups are important to talk about and experience. An historical perspective may be quite supportive in the discussions that are generated. Have guest speakers; creating a pen pal arrangement or big friend with another class or school may also facilitate the learning in this area.

These are core principles:

1. People work best when they feel valued.
2. People feel most valued when they believe that their individual and group differences have been taken into account.
3. The ability to learn from people we regard as different is the key to becoming fully empowered.
4. When people feel valued and empowered, they are enabled to build relationships in which they work together interdependently and synergistically.

Time is spent discussing the five principles in the valuing differences model with special emphasis put on number 3 followed by number 2. The emphasis is placed on learning from people we regard as different. Having a willingness to hear, listen, and respond in an affirmative manner to others—more often than not—allows us to hear and learn without constraints. Each of the valuing differences, items are important in helping people acknowledge and then work on changing their biases and prejudices. The primary goal is to get people to "own their own learning" and to experience their cultural diversity with others.

"Owning your own learning" means to be responsible and accountable for what you do, say, see, and feel about in the learning environment. It is important that students and teachers consciously decide what they are able to do and can respond to in a given situation. It is the student and teacher who must act in a self-assured and willing manner in order to try something new, something difficult, as well as something easy. It is helping to create the kind of learning environment that supports individual and group learning. It is the student and teacher being able to identify and participate in a learning environment that fosters trust.

Another exercise is a written exercise titled "Who am I?" In groups of two or three, each person must tell in writing how they perceive each other. This is done nonverbally. Once each member of the group is finished, the sharing is done verbally. If new information is disclosed, it can be added to the individual's paper. This exercise may last for thirty to forty-five minutes. This can lead into a self-esteem discussion.

CHAPTER EIGHT

Spirituality and Teacher/Student Understanding of Self

Expressing our beliefs through language, images, and relationships reveals who we are/strive to be.

—Davis-Fuller

It is imperative that as we value the levels of learning and instructing that we also acknowledge there is a spiritual side of reality to learning and knowing. It is not the religious aspects of individuals, but it is the connection that individuals and groups make to their inner feelings, beliefs, and social consciousness to intra/interrelationships with regard to self-identity. The spiritual side and integrity to learning are often not addressed at all in educational texts, journals, and articles about teaching and learning.

It is frightening for many to embark into the discussion about one's beliefs and inner feelings about a given topic or topics related to classroom curriculum. It is more than asking what one thinks about something, or what one has discovered through finding out about a theme, topic, or subject discipline. It is the essence of innate beliefs. How do we as educators express our beliefs in the cognitive world of knowing? Is there a sense of respect and acknowledgement for those who are different in language, culture, religious pursuits, age, gender, economic, and social status (not withstanding political ideology).

There are so many symbols of status and ideology that impose themselves on our physique and well-being. There are real and imagined goals to achieve and possessions to attain in the life and stages of children and adults. With all of the external variables that encompass us, we are many times not aware that we are unconscious of our being or purpose in living with relationship to what matters and is important for daily living.

In the classroom, what is it that teachers for the most part do not get about their students? What are the missing linkages that are needed to experiencing the whole child/ young adult? We want obedience and compliance, we want test scores that prove we have imparted content, we want lesson planning and implementing of plans to be successful in the delivery and understanding, we want participation in classrooms by students to be enthusiastic/sincere, we want administrators to value our work and worth, we want parents to applaud our efforts and form partnerships, we want fewer interruptions in teaching time, we want respect for our effort, we want praise when something has gone extremely well in the classroom and classroom-related activities, we want validation, and we want more compensation for what we do professionally in the classroom. The list is truly endless; and with that being stated, what can we manage for ourselves as professionals teaching in the learning environment? We must manage ourselves before we can even begin to think about managing others including our families and loved ones. Managing and coping without a spiritual base of knowing or even understanding purpose and need of ourselves to others make the notion of managing and coping become difficult at best and impossible at worse. What is it all right for students to do behaviorally in the classroom and not do in the classroom? What are the consequences for what one does or does not do? Is the concept of consequences understood by all in the classroom for teaching responsibility for one's actions? The same responsibility is an important concept to know, learn, teach, and understand. Responsibility as defined by *Merriam-Webster Dictionary* is the quality or state of being responsible as moral, legal, or mental accountability; reliability; trustworthiness; something for which one is responsible; or a burden.

Spirituality in Critical Multicultural Practice

To use a higher-education focus that lends itself to teaching and learning in the classroom, it is stated that "learners construct knowledge in different ways." The construction of new knowledge not only is related to the rational and intellectual domains typical of higher education but also is a spiritual pursuit related to learners' cultural identity, their personal experience, history, and relationship to the community (Dillard 2000). Especially for students of color and other marginalized by structural inequities based on gender, sexual orientation, and social class, it is important to have knowledge by and about members of their own communities represented in the reading (Gay 2000; Jett and Savage-Davis 2005; Sleeter 1996). Further, many authors highlight the importance of using real-life-based narratives from members of different cultural groups to make issues of cultural identity visible (Florio-Ruane 2001; Huber, Murphy, and Clandinin 2003; Phillion and Fang He 2004). This helps students explore aspects of both their own and others' cultural identity and also often leads to an exploration of how different cultural assumptions and power relations based on race and culture play out in society; it also creates greater equity in the classroom.

Second, it is also important to develop activities that potentially engage learners' spirituality as well as their cultural identity. This can happen without necessarily discussing spirituality directly; it can happen through engaging what Floria-Ruane (2001) refers to as the "cultural imagination."

When people dialogue about their cultural histories and then reshape these histories as they weave new threads of meaning about their own and others' cultural lives with earlier threads, they are engaging cultural imagination. Often such engagement is experienced by learners as a spiritual process (Tisdell 2005).

Faith development theorist, James Fowler (1981), suggested that spirituality is about how people construct knowledge through largely unconscious and symbolic processes and noted the significance of imagination in spirituality. Similarly, Parks (2000) in discussing the role of imagination in spirituality notes that it is a "composing activity" of putting together insights, images, and ideas in a way that approximates the real and that it speaks to a larger reality that is about meaning making (Multicultural Perspectives 2006, 8:23-24).

Postnote for the Notebook

Classroom managing is teaching content. It is learning and knowing how students take in information and relate it to their experiences now and in the future. It is connecting the professionals with students. It is connecting spirituality with reality and managing information. It is understanding cultural differences and similarities in individuals and groups. It is doing the "homework" and "self-exploration" required to know about ethnic and culture history and reaching out to families, communities for a cooperative and inclusion approach to teaching and learning in the classroom. It is being in the present and knowing how to project for the future (envision the future).

Teaching is solely about the children. Do not be confused, misled, deceived, or unfocused. Do not be self-indulgent or ego-centered. Parenting is a lifelong journey. We learn, we challenge, we reevaluate, we question, we move forward. Clearly, there are no quantities, but there is the possibility and real desire for our children to succeed and thrive in their lives. We are our children's role models. Our children are our teachers as well; there is no script!

Parenting, classroom managing and teaching cultural diversity are continuously being reviewed, challenged, and redefined. This list captures the essence of suppositions for teachers, students, parents, administrators, and community people.

If you open it, close it.
If you turn it on, turn it off.
If you break it, admit it.
If you can't fix it, call in someone who can.
If you borrow it, return it.
If you value it, take care of it.
If you make a mess, clean it up.
If you move it, put it back.
If it belongs to someone else, get permission to use it.
If you don't know how to operate it, leave it alone and ask questions.

Author unknown

REFERENCES

"A Brief History of Asians in America." (1990). Asian-American Resource Workshop, Boston.

Banks, James A. and Cherry A. McGee Banks, (1993) Multicultural Education Issues and Perspectives. Second edition, Allyn and Bacon, Boston 42, 43-44.

Bailey, Peter, (1990). "Self-Esteem: What It Is and How to Get Some," *Crisis Magazine*, Vo. 97, No. 10 December.

Bell, Larry I., (2002/2003). "Strategies that Close the Gap," Educational Leadership, Alexandria, Va., Association for Supervision and Curriculum Development, December/January.

Bennett, Lerome, (1962). Jr. *Before the Mayflower: A History of the Negro in America 1619-1964*, Penguin Books.

"Beyond Stereotypes: Developing Authentic Relationships with Diverse Others: Chap. Four, p 71.

Davis Fuller, Ethlyn, (1992) Cultural Diversity in the Classroom: Reaching Out to Cultural Diversity, Library of Congress Registration Number TX 462 383, Boston, January: 7.

Delpit, Lisa and Joanne Kilgour Dowdy, edit (2002). Victoria PurcellGates, The Skin That We Speak: Thoughts on Language and Culture in the Classroom, New York, The New Press.

Empleo, Arlene C., (2006). "Disassembling the Model Minority: Asian Pacific Islander Identities and Their School Experiences," Multicultural

Perspectives, Volume 8, Number 3, New Jersey, Lawrence Erlbaum Associates Publisher.

Garcia, Eugene, (2002) Student Cultural Diversity: Understanding and Meeting the Challenge, third edition, Houghton Mifflin Co., New York: 35 122.

Gay, Geneva, (1993). "Ethnic Minorities and Educational Equality," Multicultural Education: Issues and Perspectives, 2nd ed., James A. Banks and Cherry A. McGee Banks, (editors) Boston, Allyn and Bacon publishers.

George, Robert E., (2006). "The Race Card: An Interactive Tool for Teaching Multiculturalism" Multicultural Perspectives, Volume 8, number 3 New Jersey, Erlbaum Associates, Publishers.

Gratz, Donald B. (2002). "Leaving No Child Behind," commentary Education Week, June 11, 2002.

Gwin, Joseph, (1990) "Self-Esteem and Academic Excellence: Are the Two in Conflict?" *Crisis Magazine*, Vol. 97, No. 10, December: 16

Joyce, Bruce and Marsha Weil, Models of Teaching, (1986). 3rd edition, Englewood Cliffs, New Jersey, Prentice-Hall, Inc.

Kopkowski, Cynthia, (2006). "It's There: Talk About If," Neatoday, National Education Association, Volume 25 Number 3 November.

Latham, Andrew S., (1998). "Rules and Learning," Educational Leadership. September Association for Supervision and Curriculum Development.

Logan, Rayford W., Ed., W. E. B. DuBois: (1971). A Profile, American Century Series, New York, Hill and Wang.

Manuel, Diane, Boston Globe, (1991) "Self-Esteem in Girls: How Can It Be Kept High?" January 20, 1991.

Mendes, Ernest, (2003). "What Empathy Can Do," Educational Leadership, September Association for Supervision and Curriculum Development.

Moran, Seana, Mindy Kornhaber, and Howard Gardner, (2006). "Orchestrating Multiple Intelligences," Educational Leadership Vol. 64, no.1 September. http//Latinoseducation pewhispanic.org, Pew Hispanic Center Research Topics: Education (12/4/2002). "The Improving Educational Profile of Latino Immigrants" B. Lindsay Lowell and Roberto Suro.

Ravitch, Diane, (1985). *The Schools We Deserve: Reflections on the Educational Crisis of Our Times*, New York Basic Books, Inc. Publishers.

Ross-Perry, Elinor, (1998). "Addressing the Needs of Diverse Learners," *Pathways to Thinking*, Norwood, Mass., Christopher—Gordon Publishers.

Sadker, Myra and Davis Sadker, (1991) No.2 November 20 American Teacher, Vol. 76.

Silberman, Charles E. (1964). *Crisis in Black and White*, New York, Random House.

Stipek, Deborah, "Relationships Matte" (2006). Educational Leadership Vol. 64 no.1 September, Association for Supervision and Curriculum Development.

Stoskopf, Alan, (1991). "Teaching Racism in the Classroom: A Profile of Dr. Beverly Daniel Tatum's Research," Facing History and Ourselves News, February.

Tisdell, Elizabeth, (2006). "Spirituality: Cultural Identity, and Epistemology in Culturally Responsive teaching in Higher Education," Multicultural Perspectives, Volume 8, Number 3, New Jersey, Lawrence Erlbaum Associates, Publishers.

Walker, Barbara, (1989). *Valuing Differences: A Theory-Based Model for Dealing with Differences in the Workplace*, Boston, Ma., Digital Equipment Corporation.

Zanger, V.V., (1990). Drawing on Diversity: A Handbook for and by Boston Teachers in Multicultural, Multiracial Classrooms, North Zone Intercultural

Project in Collaborations with Boston University, funded through Chapter 636, Boston Public Schools.

Ziglar, Zig, (2002). revised it "Motivation and Positive Thinking," Raising Positive Kids in a Negative World, Nashville, Tenn. Thomas Nelson Publishers, Inc.,